Yummy Yarns
Knits for Kids

Yummy Yarns Knits for Kids

20 Easy-to-Knit Designs for Ages 2 to 8 Featuring Fun Novelty Yarns

Kathleen Greco and Nick Greco

Photography by Joe VanDeHatert

Watson-Guptill Publications / New York

FOR MADALYN AND WILLIAM NICHOLAS

Creative Director / Creative Editor Kathleen Greco *Dimensional Illustrators, Inc.*

Executive Editor Nick Greco *Dimensional Illustrators, Inc.*

Design and Typography Deborah Davis *Deborah Davis Design*

Knitwear Designs Kathleen Greco *Dimensional Illustrators, Inc.*

Senior Acquisitions Editor Joy Aquilino *Watson-Guptill Publications*

Fashion Photographer Joe VanDeHatert *Studio V*

Knitting and Yarn Photography Kathleen Greco *Dimensional Illustrators, Inc.*

Knitting Consultants Dr. Gail G. Cohen, Maria Williams

First published in 2005
by Watson-Guptill Publications,
a division of VNU Business Media, Inc.,
770 Broadway, New York, NY 10003
www.wgpub.com

ISBN 0-8230-5986-3

First printing, 2005

Library of Congress Control Number: 2005927856

1 2 3 4 5 6 7 8 9 / 12 11 10 09 08 07 06 05

Printed in China

Acknowledgments

We would like to express our appreciation to everyone involved in the production of this book. A warm thank you to Deborah Davis for her creative graphic design. We appreciate the impressive photography of Joe VanDeHatert and thank Wendy VanDeHatert for the children's makeup. Thank you to Joy Aquilino for her editorial guidance. We are grateful to Maria Williams from the Stitch Inn for her knitting expertise and assistance. Thanks to Gail Cohen for her excellent knitting talents, and Christen Parzych for her knitted samples. A very special thanks to our exceptional models, Edward, Madalyn, Meghan, Olivia, Thomas, William, and to their wonderful parents. We would like to acknowledge the many yarn companies for their generous contributions. Finally, all our love to our family for their unending support and encouragement.

–Nick and Kathleen Greco

Photographed at the Enchanted Woods™ at Winterthur, an American Country Estate, and Longwood Gardens, Kennett Square, Pennsylvania.

Yarn Contributors
Berroco, Inc.
Colinette Hand Dyed Yarns / distributed by Unique Kolours
Crystal Palace Yarns
Plymouth Yarn Company, Inc.
Schaefer Yarn Company
Skacel Collection, Inc.
Stitch Inn / Lahaska, PA
The Knitting Room / Medford, NJ
Trendsetter Yarns

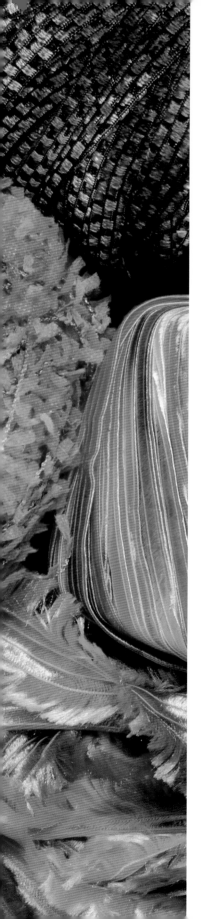

Contents

INTRODUCTION

Variety and versatility of novelty yarns make them ideal for knitting cherished garments for children. Knitting with novelty yarns is super-fun and super-easy. *Yummy Yarns Knits for Kids* will inspire your creativity and teach you the essentials of knitting with cool novelty yarns. The 20 original projects in this book, designed for kids aged two to eight are a perfect fit for today's active youngsters.

Yummy Yarns Knits for Kids introduces both first-time and long-time knitters to simple projects that feature the latest in novelty yarns. Full-color, step-by-step photographs teach you the fundamentals of knitting, including— casting on, knitting, purling, increasing, decreasing, and binding off.

For the young lady in your life, begin knitting a Candy Scarf, Jelly Flip-flops, and hip Jelly Purse. Progress to a cool Hawaiian Crop Top, Rainbow Poncho, and warm Wrap Poncho. Complete her wardrobe with a Ballerina Halter, Round Capelet, and shocking pink Fuzzy Jacket.

For the little guy in your life, knit a fun Snake Scarf, Cozy Scarf, Wool Cap, and Handsome Vest. He'll enjoy the playful Puppet Mittens, warm Easy Pullover, Suede Sweater, and Little Man Cardigan.

For all the children, we created brightly colored Fun Cushions, Fuzzy Party Pillows, and a plush Cuddle Blanket.

1 NOVELTY YARN BASICS

Novelty yarns delight us with their funky fibers, fuzzy textures, and alluring colors. Like precious gems, we savor these magnificent yarns and we are never disappointed with the exciting new offerings that we find each season. Blending different novelty yarn fibers and textures gives knitters an opportunity to produce unique handknit fabrics.

This chapter discusses the fundamentals and techniques needed to work successfully with the latest fashion yarns. Novelty yarns come in eight distinct categories: Eyelash, Fur, Fuzz, Flat, Chunky and Funky, Multi-strand, Jelly, and Hybrid yarns. Learn which yarns work best alone, or in combination with other yarns.

Knitting with novelty yarns doesn't require special training, but the techniques section offers some helpful hints that are guaranteed to give your knitwear a professional-looking finish. Learn proven techniques for keeping an accurate stitch count, creating a furry texture, ironing flat yarns, and working with multiple strands of yarn.

Combining yarns successfully adds another dimension to your knitting, and offers you unlimited possibilities. Novelty yarns are excellent for kids' knitwear because they afford you the opportunity to create colorful, fun garments that all children will enjoy wearing.

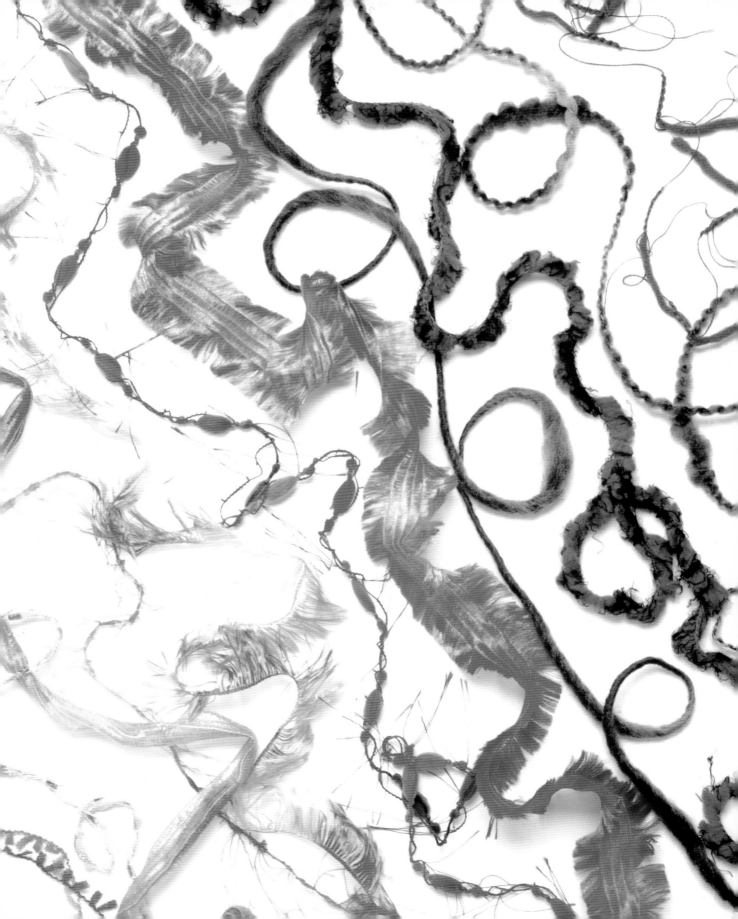

Knitting with Novelty Yarns

To achieve the best results when working with novelty yarns, we have developed several techniques that will help you untangle the complexities of working with them, and make knitting easier and more enjoyable. These methods will improve your knitting skills, build your confidence, and produce professional-looking knitwear.

Keeping an Accurate Stitch Count

When knitting with fur, fuzz or a combination of yarns, it is often difficult to see the stitches, and to keep an accurate count of the number of stitches on the needle. Stitch markers are an excellent method for monitoring your stitch count. After each cast on stitch, place a marker. When you begin the first row of stitches, simply slip the ring over to the right-hand needle. At the end of each row, count the rings on the needle.

Combing Fur Yarns

When working with fur yarns, a fine-toothed comb is your most important tool! To achieve the best fur effect, we recommend combing back and forth across the needle several times after completing each row. This technique works best with long fur yarns. The result is a fluffy fur texture that hides the knitted stitches.

Ironing Ribbon Yarns

Flat ribbon yarns can wrinkle during winding or handling. To remove wrinkles from ribbon yarn, pull the yarn gently through a large curling iron set on Low-Medium temperature. The yarn will be easier to work, and the knitted fabric will look great.

Knitting with 2 Strands or More

Sometimes a pattern calls for knitting with two strands or more. When working with two strands of the same yarn, new knitters often pull the yarn from the inside and the outside of the ball at the same time. As you pull the yarn, the ball spins and eventually the yarn gets twisted or tangled. We recommend winding two separate balls of the same yarn and separate the balls into plastic bags. This technique prevents the yarn from tangling.

Eyelash Yarns

Eyelash, one of the most popular novelty yarns, has three or more fibers spaced evenly along a core center thread. As an accent yarn, Eyelash is added to various yarns to create a wispy effect. The fibers are so thin, that virtually any color will add zest to your knitted projects. For a light, delicate fabric, hold together two or more strands of Eyelash yarn in different colors and knit them on large needles. Eyelash is also easily paired with other yarns without affecting the gauge. In the Candy Scarf for girls (page 40), we combined Eyelash yarn with Multi-strand yarn on large needles for a lacy combination.

You can also create a delicate fringe effect by knitting two strands of Eyelash yarn together. In the Ballerina Halter (page 64), we knit the first two rows of the ruffle with two strands held together to produce a ruffle with a lovely self-fringing edge.

Fur Yarns

Perfect for children's knitwear, Fur yarn is fluffy and soft, and is available in a wide palette of playful colors. Fur yarn consists of several straight poly-fibers aligned along a single base thread. There are long Fur yarns (fibers longer than 2") and short Fur yarns (fibers shorter than 2"). Both produce a thick, shaggy texture that resembles the fur of a plush stuffed animal and hides most knitting errors. This multi-purpose yarn knits up great alone, or in combination with other fibers.

In the little girls' Fuzzy Jacket (page 72), we used hot pink Fur yarn throughout. The effect is a cuddly-soft, irresistible fabric that looks great and wears well. For extra edging on the cuffs, we used two strands held together. In the Round Capelet (page 68) poncho, we created a thick lush edging by knitting four strands of white Fur yarn held together.

Fuzz Yarns

Fuzz yarn consists of multiple brushed pile fibers aligned on a base core thread. This feathery-soft, medium-weight novelty yarn is very versatile. The knitted fabric feels like mohair or cashmere, super-soft to the touch, making it a good choice for children's projects. Fuzz yarn works well, either in single or double strands. The boys' Easy Pullover (page 98) utilizes soft Fuzz yarn for the cuffs and waistband.

When paired with other yarns, Fuzz adds bulk to knitted fabric and provides support for finer yarns. The Wrap Poncho (page 60) uses synthetic mohair Fuzz with alternating stripes of Fur and Eyelash yarns. The result is a colorful combination of textures and fibers.

Flat Yarns

The category of Flat yarns comprises three different types: Ladder, Flag, and Ribbon. Ladder or railroad yarns resemble railroad tracks with two thin parallel strands of thread joined by perpendicular crossbar fibers. In Flag yarns, there are many evenly spaced colorful tuft fibers along a center core. Ribbon yarns, as the name implies, are slim flat bands of yarn.

The Hawaiian Crop Top (page 52) is knit with colorful wide Ribbon yarn. This synthetic micro-fiber is feathery-soft, and great for girl's knitwear. For the Ballerina Halter (page 64), we paired a thin, silky Ribbon yarn with a Multi-strand yarn. The result is a beautiful, supple fabric that works up into a delicate top.

Chunky and Funky Yarns

Chunky and Funky are ideal yarns for kids because they are soft, warm, and colorful. Ranging from chenille, bouclé and slubbed, Chunky novelty yarns are super-bulky and super-quick to knit. These yarns produce well-defined stitches that are easy to see, and add a soft texture to the knitted fabric.

Funky yarns are the most eclectic of all the novelty yarns. These supple yarns have uneven fibers that include bulky tufts, or a variety of random colored strands along a central core. The Little Man Cardigan (page 106) features a cheerful chunky yarn with clumps of green and blue that knits into a durable yet playful material. The Wrap Poncho (page 60) incorporates a few rows of bright squiggly yarn mixed with mohair and cotton, resulting in dynamic splashes of color. These clever yarns add volume and offer a novel slant to any project. While Chunky yarns stand up well when knitted alone, Funky yarns work best as accent yarns.

Multi-strand Yarns

Multi-strand yarns are an extraordinarily beautiful combination of two or more novelty yarns that may include Eyelash, Fuzz, and Fur. These yarns come wound with several strands twisted together. Using Multi-strand yarn can save you time, as they are already color coordinated, and they are very economical since you avoid the cost of purchasing expensive yarn skeins. These contemporary yarns are a great way for knitters to experiment with a variety of combinations of texture and contrast. Manufacturers have eliminated the hassle of bridging different gauges since all the combined yarns are compatibly matched.

A super-chunky, Multi-strand chenille yarn was used to knit the Fun Cushion tops (page 112). Thick, soft chenille was intertwined with Eyelash for a very delicate yet highly durable fabric.

Jelly Yarns

Jelly Yarn™ is one of the coolest yarns in knitting. This glossy, round plastic is available in three weights—Superfine, Fine, and Bulky—and comes in a variety of yummy colors. Knitting with Jelly Yarn™ is novel and fun, yet sturdy and flexible. We recommend knitting this yarn with metal needles, while using an even, loose tension. If you tend to knit tightly, we recommend that you wipe the needles with silicone or ArmorAll® to help the yarn glide smoothly on the needles.

In the Jelly Purse (page 48), we used Fine weight Jelly Yarn™ in a Pink Parfait color producing a slick surface texture. Translucent pink handles and a white boa complete this very chic accessory. Our Jelly Flip-flops (page 44) feature a combination of Jelly Yarn™ and sparkly glass beads.

Hybrid Yarns

What's new in novelty yarns? Hybrid yarns fuse two or more types of novelty yarn into a single strand, sometimes in more than one color. Hybrid yarns offer knitters an array of patterns and textures without the complex stitch patterns.

In the Handsome Vest project (page 90), we used a brown hybrid yarn, for the body. The yarn strand consists of a medium-weight chenille alternating with a double strand of silky ribbon yarn. When knit in the Stockinette Stitch pattern, this feature creates a random pattern in the fabric.

2 LEARNING TO KNIT

Reading a knitting pattern can be a daunting task for the first-time knitter. This chapter translates knitting jargon, clarifies abbreviations used in knitting patterns, and shows you the equipment and materials you need to successfully begin your knitting experience. If you're new to knitting, start by learning the fundamentals; making a slipknot, casting on, knitting, purling, and binding off. Through step-by-step photographs, study techniques of increasing and decreasing, which are used to knit projects with a contoured shape.

Discover the importance that needle size, gauge, and tension play in successfully completing a knitted project. Master the two fundamental knitting stitch patterns, Garter and Stockinette. Learn finishing techniques, including how to join seams, weave in loose ends, crochet a finished edge, create handmade tassels, and blocking. Finally, discover decorative stitches such as the wrap stitch and ribbing. With patience, determination, and practice, you will enjoy mastering the techniques needed to knit all the projects in this book.

Reading a Knitting Pattern

Knitting instructions provide specific information for completing a hand knit garment. A pattern will include yarn, needles, sizes, gauge, stitch patterns, and row-by-row instructions for completing the pattern. With practice you will be able to read instructions easily.

Yarn

Knitting patterns will include the amount, name, yardage, weight, content, and color of the yarn needed to complete the project.

Needles

Needles come in size US #0 (2.00mm) to size US #50 (25.50mm). The needle size will determine the gauge of your knitted fabric (page 32). Small needles produce smaller stitches, while large needles produce larger stitches. We recommend practicing the skills in this chapter with #15 needles and a solid-color, super-bulky yarn.

Finished Sizes

Projects that include instructions for multiple sizes show alternate measurements in parentheses (see "Symbols," below).

Gauge

Refer to page 32 for information.

Symbols

***Asterisks** mark the start of patterns that are to be worked more than one time.

[ ] **Brackets** are sometimes substituted for asterisks. [K3, P2] 4 times means, Knit 3 stitches, Purl 2 stitches a total of 4 times.

( ) **Parentheses** indicate size, number of stitches or inches. Sizes: 2 (4, 6, 8), Stitches: 16 (18, 22, 24) or inches: 8 (10, 12, 14)". Patterns are written in parentheses according to size from smallest to largest. Fits chest sizes 13 (14, 15, 16)"/33 (36, 38, 41)cm.

Needle Sizes

U.S.	Metric	U.S.	Metric	U.S.	Metric
0	2.00mm	7	4.50mm	15	10.00mm
1	2.25mm	8	5.00mm	17	12.75mm
2	2.75mm	9	5.50mm	18	14.00mm
3	3.25mm	10	6.00mm	19	15.00mm
4	3.50mm	10.5	6.50mm	35	19.00mm
5	3.75mm	11	8.00mm	50	25.50mm
6	4.00mm	13	9.00mm		

Knitting Abbreviations

To save space, knitting patterns are written in abbreviations. Remember to read each pattern completely before you begin knitting.

approx – approximately
beg – begin
BO – bind off
cm – centimeter(s)
CO – cast on
cont – continue
dec – decrease
Garter st – K every row
gm – gram
inc – increase
" or **in** – inch(es)
K – knit
K1 tbl – knit one stitch through back loop
k2tog – knit 2 stitches together
kfb – knit into front and back of same stitch
LH – left hand
mm – millimeter
P – purl
patt – pattern
pfb – purl into front and back of same stitch

psso – pass slipped stitch over
p2tog – purl 2 stitches together
p2tog tbl – purl 2 stitches together through back loop
rep – repeat
rep from * – repeat instruction after *
RH – right hand
rev St st – reverse stockinette stitch (purl 1 row, knit 1 row)
rnd – round
sl st – slip stitch
Sl1 K – slip 1 stitch knitwise
Sl1 P – slip 1 stitch purlwise
Sl1, K1, PSSO or SKP – slip 1 stitch, knit 1 stitch, pass slipped stitch over
st(s) – stitch(es)
St st – stockinette stitch (K 1 row, P 1 row)
tbl – through back loop
tog – together
work even – continue in pattern without increasing or decreasing
WS – wrong side
wyib – with yarn in back (knit stitch)
wyif – with yarn in front (purl stitch)
YO – yarn over

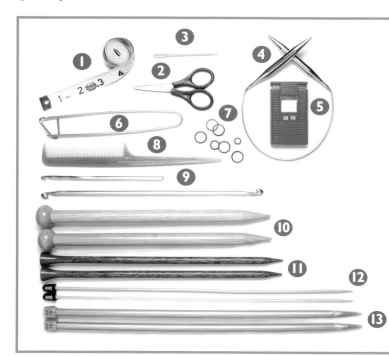

Essential Materials

1. Measuring Tape
2. Scissors
3. Tapestry Needle
4. Circular Needles #13 (6mm)
5. Stitch Counter
6. Stitch Holder
7. Ring Markers
8. Novelty Yarn Comb
9. Crochet Hooks
10. Wood Knitting Needles #19 (15mm)
11. Wood Knitting Needles #13 (9mm)
12. Metal Knitting Needles #5 (3.75mm)
13. Plastic Knitting Needles #15 (10mm)

Slipknot

To begin knitting, you need to make a slipknot. Tie the knot firmly on the needle, but not tight enough to prevent the stitch from sliding easily along the needle.

1. Begin a slipknot by winding the yarn around your index and middle fingers two times.

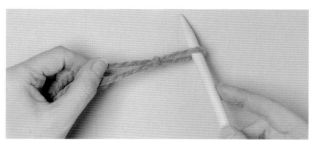

2. Pull the yarn attached to the ball through the loop and create a new loop.

3. Tighten the knot on the needle. The slipknot becomes the first stitch on the needle.

Double Cast On

Casting on adds the first row of stitches called for in the pattern. The double cast on method uses a tail and the strand attached to the ball to cast on the required number of stitches. The knitting symbol for casting on is **CO**.

1. Wrap the tail clockwise around your left thumb and the ball yarn clockwise around your left index finger to form a slingshot. Hold the tail and ball yarn firmly in the palm of your left hand.

2. Insert the needle under the yarn on your thumb from bottom to top.

3. Insert the needle behind the yarn on your index finger from top to bottom, bring the needle through the loop of yarn on your thumb, and slip your thumb off the loop. Repeat steps 2 and 3.

Handle Cast On

Use this technique with Jelly Yarn™ to cast on purse handles (page 48) and flip-flops (page 44). Begin with a tail 3 times the width of the handle area. Next, wipe metal needles with ArmorAll® so needles glide easily.

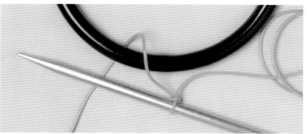

1. Make a slipknot and pass the tail of the yarn to the back of the needle. Wrap the handle from front to back and pull it snug.

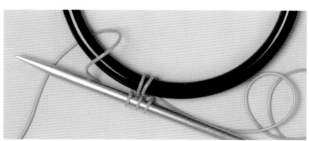

2. Cast on the next stitch using the double cast on method. Pass the tail of the yarn to the back of the needle. Wrap the handle from front to back.

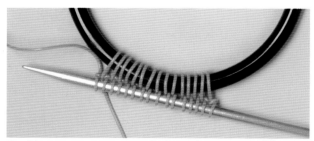

3. Alternate 1 cast on stitch and 1 wrapped loop until desired number is achieved. Make all stitches and wrapped loops with uniform tension.

Circular Needles

Circular needles consist of a pair of short needles joined by a flexible nylon cord. They are ideal for knitting tubular items such as hats and socks, and can also be used in place of straight needles to accommodate a large number of stitches.

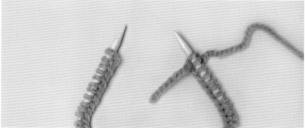

1. Cast on the number of stitches called for in the pattern. The needle holding the first cast on stitch should be in your left hand.

2. Align the ridge of each cast on stitch on the inside of the needle to ensure the stitches are not twisted. Place a ring marker on the RH needle.

3. Slip ring marker onto the RH needle at the end of each round. Create a Stockinette Stitch pattern by knitting every round.

Knit Stitch

The knit stitch is the most basic stitch in knitting. When making a knit stitch, always keep the yarn in back of the needles. The knitting symbol for the knit stitch is **K**.

Purl Stitch

The purl stitch is the second most popular stitch in knitting. When making a purl stitch, always keep the yarn in front of the needles. The knitting symbol for the purl stitch is **P**.

1. With the yarn in your right hand and the needle with the stitches in your left hand, insert the RH needle through the first cast on stitch from left to right (knitwise).

1. With the yarn in front and the needle with the stitches in your left hand, insert the RH needle through the first stitch from right to left (purlwise).

2. Remember to keep the yarn in back of the work for a knit stitch. Wrap the yarn counterclockwise around the tip of the RH needle.

2. The right needle is above the left needle and forms an X. Wrap the yarn counterclockwise around the tip of the RH needle.

3. Draw the tip of the RH needle up through the cast on stitch and slide the original stitch off the LH needle. Repeat steps 1, 2, and 3 until all the knit stitches are on the RH needle.

3. Draw the tip of the RH needle back through the stitch and slide the original stitch off the LH needle. Repeat steps 1, 2, and 3 until all the purl stitches are on the RH needle.

Bar Increasing

The bar increase method adds stitches and enables you to widen and shape the garment to fit properly. When you add a stitch using this method, a horizontal bar appears below the added stitch. This increase should be made at the beginning or end of a row. With this technique you knit into the front and back of the same stitch. The knitting symbol for increasing is **inc**.

Knitwise

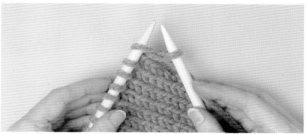

1. Insert the right hand needle (knitwise) and knit as usual but do not slip the stitch off the LH needle.

2. Insert the needle into the back of the same stitch from right to left. Wrap the yarn counterclockwise around the RH needle and draw the yarn back through the stitch.

3. Slip the original stitch off the LH needle. You have created two new knit stitches on the RH needle.

Purlwise

1. Insert the right hand needle (purlwise) and purl as usual but do not slip the stitch off the LH needle.

2. Insert the needle into the back of the same stitch from right to left. Wrap the yarn counterclockwise around the RH needle and draw the yarn back through the stitch.

3. Slip the original stitch off the LH needle. You have created two new purl stitches on the RH needle.

Decreasing

The right-slanting decreasing method—knit 2 stitches together—produces stitches that slant to the right. The knitting symbol for this decrease is **K2tog**.

The left-slanting decreasing method—slip 1 stitch, knit 1 stitch, and pass the slipped stitch over—produces stitches that slant to the left. The knitting symbol for this decrease is **Sl1, K1, PSSO**.

Right-Slanting Decrease

1. Insert the tip of the RH needle (knitwise) from left to right into the next two stitches.

2. Knit as usual with yarn in back. K2tog.

3. Slip the original stitches off the LH needle. The two stitches have been reduced to one stitch on the RH needle. The result is a right-slanting decrease.

Left-Slanting Decrease

1. Slip the first stitch knitwise off the LH needle.

2. Knit the next stitch.

3. Lift the slipped stitch up over the knit stitch and off the RH needle. The result is a left slanting-decrease.

Wrap Stitch

For the Hawaiian Crop Top (page 52), use a wrap stitch technique to create a pattern of dropped stitches. Make this decorative technique by knitting one stitch and wrapping the yarn twice around the right hand needle. Repeat across the row.

1. Knit one and wrap the yarn counterclockwise around the RH needle two times. Repeat across the row.

2. Knit one and slip the two wrapped loops off the LH needle. Repeat across the row.

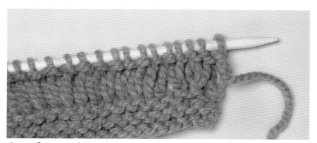

3. After each unwrapped stitch row, hold the stitches on the needle, and tug gently on the knitting to straighten the dropped stitches.

Binding Off

To prevent the knitted fabric from unraveling, you must bind off. This method secures the stitches on your knitwear and leaves a clean, decorative edge. The knitting symbol for binding off is **BO**.

1. Knit the first two stitches.

2. Insert the tip of the LH needle knitwise into the first stitch. Lift the stitch up over the second stitch and off the RH needle.

3. Knit one stitch and repeat step 2 until one stitch remains on the needle. Slide the last stitch off the needle, weave the yarn through the stitch, and knot to secure.

Tension and Gauge

Tension

The word tension refers to how tight or how loose your stitches are on the needle. The tension in your knitting has a direct relationship to the finished size of the garment you are knitting. Always knit a 4" (10cm) square test swatch to check your stitch tension. Adjust the needle size to match the recommended gauge.

Gauge

Gauge is the number of stitches and rows over a standard measurement, usually 4" (10cm). Always follow the recommended gauge and needle size to ensure your garment fits properly. **Remember: Always take time to check your gauge.**

Using identical yarns, we cast on 18 stitches and knit 30 rows. The only difference is needle size. The importance of testing your gauge can never be underestimated. Before you begin knitting a project, knit a 4" (10cm) x 4" (10cm) test swatch using the needle size and yarn weight as directed in the pattern.

Joining Yarns

As you follow a knitting pattern, you will run out of yarn, want to switch yarn, or change colors. To prevent the stitches from bulging, you should join yarn at the end of a row. This will allow you to weave the yarn ends into a seam when you finish the project.

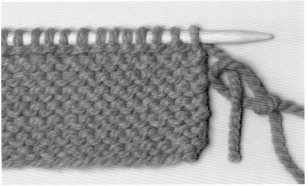

1. Tie a slipknot loosely around the old yarn leaving a 6" (15cm) tail.

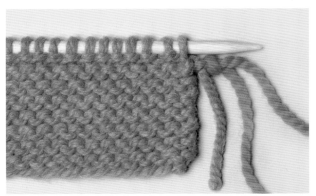

2. Slide the knot up next to the edge of the work and continue knitting.

Weaving Ends

When your garment is complete, you will need to hide all loose ends caused by casting on, binding off, changing yarn, or changing colors. For a professional look, untie all knots and weave yarn ends into the seam of your garment. This will prevent unraveling and add strength.

1. Thread the yarn end through a tapestry needle.

2. Insert the needle through the loops along the edge of the knitted work, and trim the end of the yarn close to the surface.

Blocking

Once your handmade garment is sewn together, we recommend you block it to achieve the correct dimensions. Blocking controls the shape of your knitted garment, helps even out stitches, and prevents the knitted piece from curling, or shrinking. It allows you to make adjustments to the final shape and size, and helps flatten any bulging seams caused by joining the fabric.

Before you block your finished project, read the yarn label and follow the blocking instructions for the yarn used to knit it. We do not recommend blocking fuzz or fur novelty yarns.

Use a blocking board and rustproof pins to pin your garment to the desired size and dimension. The pins will keep the knitted garment in its proper shape until it dries. Dampen with a spray bottle or steam, and cover with a towel until the fabric is completely dry.

Joining Seams

Seaming joins knitted fabrics together. Use the same garment yarn to join knitted pieces. If substituting yarn, choose one with similar fiber content and gauge.

We recommend using the Mattress Stitch, also called the Invisible Seam, because it produces an elastic, nearly undetectable seam.

1. Align the two knitted pieces side by side, thread a needle leaving a 6" (15cm) tail, and insert the needle between the two bottom corner stitches from back to front.

2. Insert the needle just below the horizontal bar that connects the two stitches on the right side and exit just above the same bar.

3. Insert the needle between the same two bottom stitches on the left side to secure the yarn. Repeat, inserting the needle below and above the horizontal bar on alternating sides until knitted pieces are sewn together.

4. Pull yarn ends to join seams together and weave in loose ends.

Crocheted Edges

Crocheting is fun and adds a finishing touch to necklines, collars, edges, and cuffs. Crochet hooks come in various sizes. Use the crochet hook size recommended in the pattern.

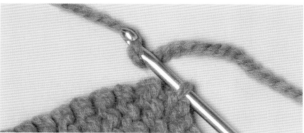

1. Insert a crochet hook in the first edge stitch, wind the yarn over the hook and draw up a loop.

2. Insert the hook into the next stitch, draw up a second loop, and wrap the yarn over the hook.

3. Pull the yarn through both loops on hook. Continue along the edge until all the stitches are crocheted.

Tassels

Tassels add a decorative element to pillows, scarves, and blankets. Use a different color yarn to give your tassels a striking contrast from the original project. All you need is some yarn, a tapestry needle, and a piece of cardboard.

1. Wind the yarn around a 3" (8cm) rectangular piece of cardboard or plastic.

2. Insert a tapestry needle with a strand of yarn under all the loops of yarn and make a tight knot.

3. Wrap a second strand of yarn about 1" (2.5cm) from the top and tie securely with a knot. Cut the loops of yarn at the bottom of the tassel and trim evenly.

Garter and Stockinette Stitch Patterns

The two basic stitches in knitting are Knit and Purl. In patterns, the Knit stitch is represented by **K** and the Purl stitch is represented by **P**. Once you have cast stitches on the needle, you can begin knitting these two stitches in various combinations called for in the pattern. Two of the knitting patterns introduced in this book are the Garter Stitch Pattern (knit every row or purl every row) and the Stockinette Stitch Pattern (knit one row, purl one row). A knitted piece created in a Garter stitch is identical on both sides. A knitted piece created in a Stockinette stitch is smooth on the right side (V-shaped stitches) and bumpy on the wrong side. The right side of a sweater is the side worn on the outside.

In the Reverse Stockinette Pattern, you purl one row and knit one row. The result of this pattern is a fabric that is bumpy on the right side and smooth on the wrong side. While learning to knit, we recommend practicing with the Garter Stitch Pattern.

Garter Stitch Pattern

Knit every row.

Stockinette Stitch Pattern (RS)

Row 1: K across. Row 2: P across.
Repeat rows 1 and 2.

Reverse Stockinette Pattern

Row 1: P across. Row 2: K across.
Repeat rows 1 and 2.

Ribbing Stitch Patterns

Single and double ribbing patterns are created by alternating knitting and purling stitches in the same row, so that you purl the stitches that you knit in the previous row, and you knit the stitches that you purled in the previous row.

These patterns are ideal for cuffs, waistbands, and bottom edges because they give the garment a finished edge and are very resilient. Ribbing should be worked on smaller needles. For single ribbing patterns, cast on an even number of stitches and *K1, P1; repeat from * to the end of the row. For double ribbing patterns, *K2, P2; repeat from * to the end of the row.

Rib 1 x 1

Cast on an even number of stitches.
Row 1: *K1, P1. Repeat from * to end of row.
Repeat this row.

Rib 2 x 2

Cast on stitches in multiples of 4.
Row 1: *K2, P2. Repeat from * to end of row.
Repeat this row.

3 KNITS FOR GIRLS

Whether you're a long-time or first-time knitter, gather your needles and yarn, and let's start knitting. Each girl is a unique young lady— so why not create something that is as individual as she is?

The first project, the Candy Scarf, is worked in a simple Garter Stitch Pattern featuring a shimmering eyelash yarn combined with a hybrid novelty yarn and accented with glass beads. Jelly Yarn™ is the newest rage in knitting. The Jelly Flip-flops and Jelly Purse reveal the fun and versatility of this super-cool, vinyl yarn. The beauty of wide ribbon yarn is showcased in the feathery Hawaiian Crop Top.

This collection would not be complete without a versatile poncho. We feature three of the season's most preferred wraps. Begin with a basic Rainbow Poncho with fringe, progress to the spectacular orange Wrap Poncho made with a combination of blended mohair and cotton, then add a colorful Round Capelet knit on circular needles. Enhance your little girl's wardrobe with a Ballerina Halter featuring an eyelash ruffle with pink rosette bows. Advance to a shocking pink Fuzzy Jacket, guaranteed to be the hit of the party. This sassy bolero top is worked with a blended soft fur yarn to create an irresistibly furry texture.

Candy Scarf

Beautiful and easy, this delicate fashion scarf is knit on big needles in a fast-finishing Garter Stitch Pattern. Iridescent yarn combined with tufts of fibers twisted with eyelash creates a light and airy fabric. Girls will love the shiny glass-beaded fringe, which makes a sweet embellishment.

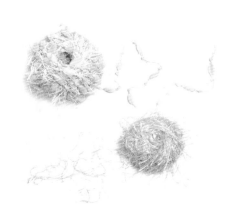

Yarn

2 balls *Trendsetter Yarns* Perla *84yds (76m) / 20g (100% polyester)* Color: #55

2 balls *Trendsetter Yarns* Bugia *85yds (78m) / 50g (100% nylon)* Color: #770

1 ball fine cotton yarn

Needles

US #19 (15mm) needles or size needed to obtain gauge.

Materials

1 darning needle

72 glass beads (6mm) *Colors: Fuchsia and Pink*

Finished Measurements

Measures 3.5" (9cm) wide x 30 (40, 50, 60)"/76 (101.5, 127, 152)cm long.

Gauge

In Garter Stitch Pattern, 10 sts and 7.5 rows = 4" (10cm) with 2 strands of Perla and 1 strand of Bugia held tog.

Garter Stitch Pattern

Knit every row.

Easy

NOTES

- As yarn can slip easily, hold two strands of eyelash yarn together firmly.
- Pull fibers out gently for fluffy effect.
- Make sure darning needle fits through glass bead hole.
- You can substitute your favorite eyelash yarn for the body of the scarf or any fine cotton yarn to make the fringe.

Scarf

Working 2 strands of Perla and 1 strand of Bugia held tog, CO 9 sts. Work Garter Stitch Pattern all rows for 30 (40, 50, 60)"/76 (101.5, 127, 152)cm or desired length. BO loosely.

Beaded Fringe

Thread 7 glass beads of alternating color on a 7" (18cm) strand of cotton yarn. Tie a knot at the top and bottom of the beaded column and attach one end through end of scarf. Place 7 beaded columns evenly at each end of the finished scarf.

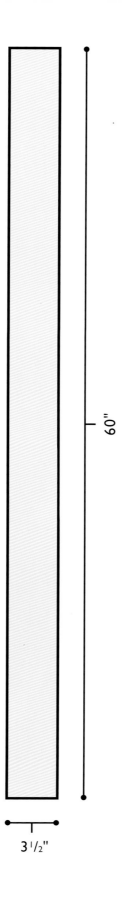

60"

3 ¹/₂"

Color Variation

Knit as pattern above. Substitute Bugia *Color: #1012* for Bugia *Color: #770*. Substitute Perla *Color: #58* for Perla *Color: #55*.

Jelly Flip-flops

Beachwear has never looked better than with these hot pink beaded Flip-flops, worked with waterproof Jelly Yarn™. We used #5 metal needles and glass beads to create these one-of-a-kind, all-weather accessories. Girls can wear them all day on the beach, in the water, or at night on the boardwalk. Simply sensational!

Yarn
1 ball *Yummy Yarns* Fine Jelly Yarn™ *85yds (78m) / (100% vinyl)*
Color: Hot Pink Candy

Needles
US #5 (3.75mm) needles or size needed to obtain gauge.

Materials
1 pair Flip-flops
300 raspberry lined crystal beads (6mm)

Sizes
2 (4, 6, 8) yrs of age. Instructions are for smallest size, with changes for other sizes in parentheses.

Finished Measurements
Measures 3.5 (3.5, 4.5, 4.5)"/9 (9, 10, 10)cm long x 1" (2.5)cm wide.

Gauge
In Garter Stitch Pattern, 32 sts and 24 rows = 4" (10cm).

Garter Stitch Pattern
Knit every row.

Easy

NOTES
• Metal needles work best with jelly yarn.
• Use ArmorAll® or silicone to help jelly yarn glide on needles easily.

Right Strap (knit one side on each right strap)
String 72" (1.8m) of cast on yarn with 60 (60, 75, 75) beads, CO 21 (21, 30, 30) sts beginning at the lower (heel) right strap. Use the Handle Cast On technique (page 27) by alternating casting on the needle and wrapping the Jelly Yarn™ around the plastic strap. Following the last cast on st, knot the tail and ball yarn tog to secure the last st on the strap.

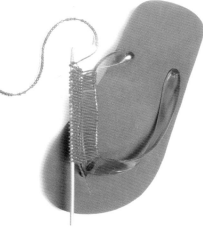

Row 1: K across.

Row 2: * Place bead, K1, repeat from *. Make sure each bead is at the back of the work before knitting each st.

Row 3: K across.

Row 4: * Place bead, K1, repeat from *. Make sure each bead is at the back of the work before knitting each st.

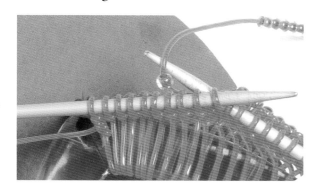

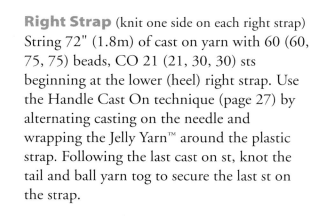

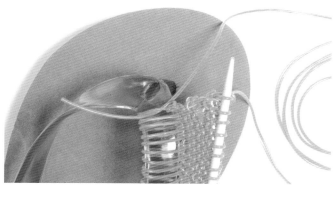

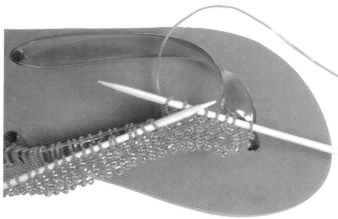

Row 5: K across.

Row 6: * Place bead, K1, repeat from *. Make sure each bead is at the back of the work before knitting each st.

Row 7: Cut 72" (1.8m) from ball. K1, * weave end of yarn through 1st loop on strap, K1. Repeat from * across the entire row. BO. Tie a knot and weave end under strap.

Left Strap (knit one side on each left strap)
Knit as for right strap, but begin CO at upper (toe) left strap.

3¹/₂ (3¹/₂, 4¹/₂, 4¹/₂)"

1"

Jelly Purse

The latest in tween-age accessories, this ritzy jelly purse is all the rage! The bag is knit in one piece and sewn with two side seams for quick assembly. Use fine pink Jelly Yarn™ and translucent pink round handles for a slick look. The white marabou boa lends a touch of chic!

Yarn

2 balls *Yummy Yarns* Fine Jelly Yarn™ *85yds (78m) / (100% vinyl) Color: Pink Parfait*

Needles

US #10 (6mm) needles or size needed to obtain gauge.

Materials

5" (12.5cm) clear pink purse ring handles

5' (1.52m) white marabou feather boa

Finished Measurements

Measures 8.5" (21.5cm) wide x 6" (15cm) long.

Gauge

In Garter Stitch Pattern, 14 sts and 24 rows = 4" (10cm) with 2 strands of fine Jelly Yarn™ held tog.

Garter Stitch Pattern

Knit every row.

Beginner

- Metal needles work best with jelly yarn.
- Use ArmorAll® or silicone to make needles glide easily.
- Do not block.

Front and Back (one piece)

Beginning with 54" (1.3m) from the tail end of the yarn, CO 15 sts working two strands of Fine Jelly Yarn™ held tog. Use the Handle Cast On technique (page 27) by alternating casting on the needle and wrapping the yarn around the plastic ring handle with the tail end.

Note: There will be yarn remaining after casting on. Wind between fingers and tie to prevent unraveling. Use to sew side seams.

Row 1: K across.

Rows 2–5: Inc 2 sts at the beg of each row, K across.

Rows 6–11: Inc 1 st at the beg of each row, K across.

Rows 12–34: K across.

Row 35: P across.

Row 36: K across.

Row 37: P across.

Row 38: K across.

Rows 39–61: K across.

Rows 62–67: Dec 1 st at the beg of each row, K across.

Rows 68–72: Dec 2 sts at the beg of each row, K across. (15 sts)

Row 73: Cut 70" (1.8m) of jelly yarn from ball. K1, loop yarn clockwise through ring, handle, end K1.

BO loosely leaving a 15" (38cm) tail of yarn for sewing the side seams.

5"

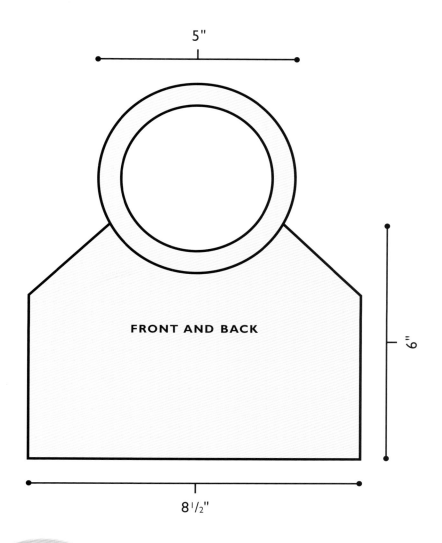

FRONT AND BACK

6"

8¹/₂"

Finishing

Sew side seams with remaining bind off and cast on Jelly Yarn™ tails. Using monofilament thread, sew boa around edge of purse twice. Make sure boa is securely attached to bag.

Hawaiian Crop Top

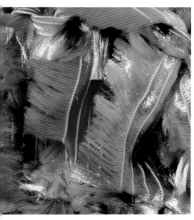

This tropical top is knit with colorful wide ribbon yarn. As the name implies, Parrot yarn is feathery and super soft. The top uses a wrap stitch that makes it quick and easy to knit. Lightweight and fun, it is ideal for afternoon parties or cool summer evenings at the seashore. Learn the Wrap Stitch on page 31.

Yarn

3 (3,4,4) balls *Plymouth Yarn* Parrot *28yds (26m) / 50g (100% nylon) Color: #1*

Needles

US #11 (8mm) needles or size needed to obtain gauge.

Sizes

2 (4, 6, 8) yrs of age. Instructions are for smallest size, with changes for other sizes in parentheses.

Finished Measurements

Chest: 26 (28, 30, 32)"/66 (71, 76, 81)cm.

Total Length: 13 (14, 15, 16)"/33 (35.5, 38, 40.5)cm.

Gauge

In Garter Stitch Pattern, 8 sts and 16 rows = 4" (10cm).

Garter Stitch Pattern

Knit every row.

Beginner

NOTES

• To remove wrinkles in ribbon yarn, iron or pull through a curling iron.

• For best results, make sure you wrap the ribbon yarn flat around the needle.

• After each Wrap Stitch row, hold the stitches on the needle and tug gently on the knitting to straighten the wrapped stitches.

• You can substitute any feathery microfiber flat ribbon yarn for the top in the same gauge.

Front and Back (two identical pieces)

CO 26 (28, 30, 32) sts.

Rows 1–4: K across.

Row 5: K1, wrap yarn 2x around needle, repeat to end of row.

Row 6: K1, unwrap loops, repeat to end of row.

Rows 7–8: K across.

Row 9: K1, wrap yarn 3x around needle, repeat to end of row.

Row 10: K1, unwrap loops, repeat to end of row.

Rows 11–12: K across.

Repeat rows 9–12, 2 (3, 4, 5) times.

K across next 2 rows. BO 3 (3, 4, 4) sts very loosely. K 4 (4, 4, 4,) sts. There will be 5 (5, 5, 5) sts on right hand needle. Attach new yarn. BO center 10 (12, 12, 14) sts. K to end.

Next row BO 3 (3, 4, 4) sts. There will be 5 (5, 5, 5) sts for each shoulder. Knit remaining shoulder strap to end of row.

Shape Neck and Shoulders

Work both sides of shoulder straps. K1, wrap 2x around needle, repeat to end of row. K1, unwrap loops, repeat to end of row. Knit 2 rows. BO loosely.

Finishing

Position shoulder seams together and sew using the Mattress Stitch (page 34) and Parrot yarn. Repeat for side seams.

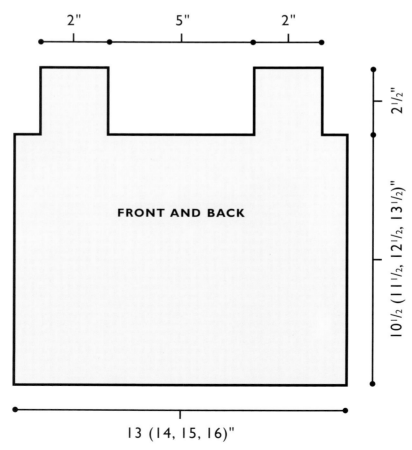

2"   5"   2"

2½"

FRONT AND BACK

10½ (11½, 12½, 13½)"

13 (14, 15, 16)"

Rainbow Poncho

The multi-color plush Rainbow Poncho is worked on super large needles in a basic Garter Stitch Pattern using Ribbon and Chunky slubbed yarn. Knit two quick-and-easy squares, sew sides, and attach strands of vibrant Fun yarn to create a playful fringed edge. Accent the folded collar with a ceramic button. Very cool!

Yarn

1 (2,2,2,2) hanks *Ironstone Yarns* Fun *80yds (73m) / 100g (85% nylon, 15% silk) Color: #112*

1 (2,2,2,2) balls *Tahki* Poppy *81yds (74m) / 50g (28% cotton, 27% acrylic, 45% nylon) Color: #001*

Needles

US #35 (19mm) needles or size needed to obtain gauge.
Size K crochet hook.

Materials

1 ceramic button

Sizes

2, (4, 6, 8) yrs of age. Instructions are for smallest size, with changes for other sizes in parentheses.

Finished Measurements

Measures 14 (16, 18, 18)"/35.5 (40.5, 45.5, 45.5)cm wide x 14 (16, 18, 18)"/35.5 (40.5, 45.5, 45.5)cm long.

Gauge

In Garter Stitch Pattern, 5.5 sts and 8 rows = 4" (10cm) with 1 strand of Fun and Poppy held tog.

Garter Stitch Pattern

Knit every row.

Easy

NOTES

- For Poppy yarn, pull fibers out gently.
- Block poncho.
- For a smaller fit, shrink in dryer on high heat for 3 minutes.
- You can substitute any chunky slubbed yarn for the poncho in the same gauge.

Front and Back (two identical pieces)

Working 1 strand of Fun and Poppy yarns held tog, CO 19 (22, 25, 25) sts.

K across for 14 (16, 18, 18)"/35.5 (40.5, 45.5, 45.5)cm. BO loosely.

Fringe

Fold Fun yarn at thinnest point and cut into 3.5" (9cm) lengths. With size K crochet hook, loop through first stitch at end of poncho. Repeat equally along the left and right edges. Trim evenly to 3" (7.5cm).

Finishing

Place two knitted squares on top of each other. Sew side "A" from upper right corner for 11 (12, 14, 14)"/28 (30.5, 35.5, 35.5)cm. Sew side "B" from lower left corner up for 11 (12, 14, 14)"/28 (30.5, 35.5, 35.5)cm. Fold down corner to form collar. Sew on button at point of collar through two layers of fabric.

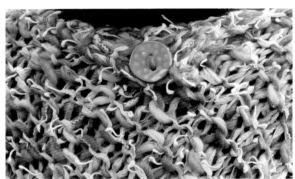

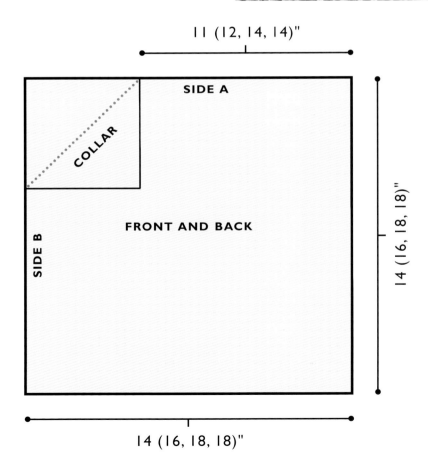

11 (12, 14, 14)"

SIDE A

COLLAR

SIDE B

FRONT AND BACK

14 (16, 18, 18)"

14 (16, 18, 18)"

Wrap Poncho

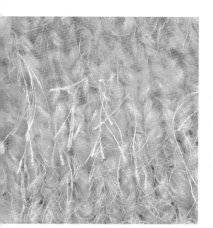

This unique design combines fashion elements of a poncho and a wrap. To make this unique project, knit a long rectangle, fold, and sew together. Work with three strands of mohair and cotton yarns, then add accents of Fur, Funky or Eyelash yarns for stripes of colorful texture. Experiment with your favorite novelties.

Yarn
1 (2,2,2) skeins *Patons* Divine *142yds (131m) / 100g (79.5% acrylic, 18% mohair, 2.5% polyester) Color: #06605*

1 (2,2,2) skeins *King Tut* Cotton *182yds (168m) / 100g (100% cotton) Color: #8000*

1 (1,1,1) ball each *Crystal Palace Yarns* Fizz *120yds (110m) / 50g (100% polyester) Colors: #9224 Key Lime and #9220 Orangeade*

1 (1,1,1) ball *Crystal Palace Yarns* Squiggle *100yds (92m) / 50g (50% polyester, 50% nylon) Color: #4705 Pippin Green*

1 (2,2,2) balls *Trendsetter Yarns* Perla *84yds (78m) / 20g (100% polyester) Color: #55*

Needles
One pair each of US #10.5 (6.5mm) and US #15 (10mm) needles or size needed to obtain gauge.

Materials
1 large button 1.5" (3.81cm) in diameter

Sizes
2 (4, 6, 8) yrs of age. Instructions are for smallest size, with changes for other sizes in parentheses.

Finished Measurements
Measures 15.5 (18, 20.5, 23)"/39.5 (45.5, 52, 58.5)cm wide x 14 (17, 20, 23)"/35.5 (43, 51, 58.5)cm long when folded.

Gauge
In Stockinette Stitch Pattern, with larger needles, 8.5 sts and 12 rows = 4" (10cm) with 1 strand of Divine and Cotton held tog.

Beginner

NOTES
- Make sure to hold onto the accent yarns, they can slip easily.
- Pull fibers out gently for a fluffy effect.
- You can substitute any mohair or cotton yarn for the poncho in the same gauge.
- To create the stripes, use any accent novelty yarn that will not alter the gauge.

Stockinette Stitch Pattern

Row 1: K across.

Row 2: P across.

Repeat rows 1 and 2.

Front and Back (one piece)

With US #10.5 needles working 1 strand of Divine and Cotton held tog, CO 57 (68, 79, 90) sts. Work in Garter Stitch Pattern for 6 rows.

Change to US #15 needles, add 1 strand of Orangeade Fizz, you are now working with three strands, and increase 15 sts across the next row = 72 (83, 94, 115) sts. Work in St st for 4 (4, 6, 6) rows.

Drop the strand of Orangeade Fizz and add 1 strand of Perla. Work 4 (4, 6, 6) rows. Drop the strand of Perla and add 1 strand of Lime Fizz. Work 4 (4, 6, 6) rows.

Drop the strand of Lime Fizz and add 1 strand of Green Squiggle. Work 2 (2, 4, 4) rows.

Drop the strand of Green Squiggle and add 1 strand of Orangeade Fizz. Work 4 (4, 6, 6) rows.

Drop the strand of Orangeade Fizz and add 1 strand of Perla. Work 4 (4, 6, 6) rows.

Drop the strand of Perla and add 1 strand of Lime Fizz. Work 4 (4, 6, 6) rows.

Last row drop the strand of Lime Fizz, work 1 strand each of Divine, Cotton, and 2 strands of Perla held tog, in Garter Stitch Pattern for 4 rows. BO loosely.

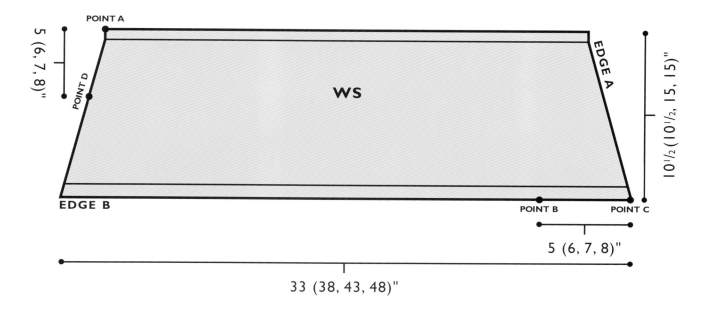

POINT A

5 (6, 7, 8)"

POINT D

WS

EDGE A

$10\frac{1}{2} (10\frac{1}{2}, 15, 15)$"

EDGE B

POINT B   POINT C

5 (6, 7, 8)"

33 (38, 43, 48)"

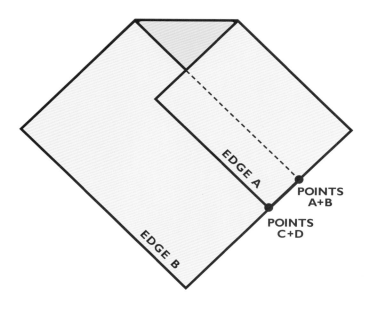

EDGE A

POINTS A+B

POINTS C+D

EDGE B

Finishing

Step 1: To form wrap poncho (WS) fold point A to point B.

Step 2: Fold point C to Point D. Position Edge A parallel to Edge B, above Squiggle stripe. Sew along Edge A to form poncho. Sew length CD and AB together. Sew button in center neck area of poncho.

Ballerina Halter

This precious halter is knit with a Multi-strand yarn paired with a silky Ribbon yarn that blend to form a delicate pastel texture of pink, yellow, and blue. The ruffle is knit with sparkly Eyelash on circular needles to accommodate all the stitches. Pink rosette bows add a final touch to an outfit fit for your little ballerina.

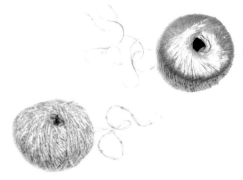

Yarn

2 (2,3,3) balls *Trendsetter Yarns* Montage *110yds (102m) / 50g (60% polyamide, 35% viscose, 5% polyester) Color: #1141*

2 (2,3,3) balls *Katia* Sevilla *153yds (141m) / 50g (100% polyamid) Color: #30*

2 (2,2,2) balls *Trendsetter Yarns* Perla *84yds (78m) / 20g (100% polyester) Color: #55*

Needles

US #10 (6mm) straight needles and US #10 (6mm) 29" (74cm) circular needles or size needed to obtain gauge.

Materials

1 large pink rosette bow and 6 small pink rosette bows

1 yard (.914m) of pink satin ribbon

Sizes

2 (4, 6, 8) yrs of age. Instructions are for smallest size, with changes for other sizes in parentheses.

Finished Measurements

Chest: 30 (32, 34, 36)"/76 (81, 86, 91)cm.

Total Length: 12 (13, 14, 15)"/30.5 (33, 35.5, 38)cm.

Gauge

In Stockinette Stitch Pattern, 16 sts and 24 rows = 4" (10cm).

Stockinette Stitch Pattern

Row 1: K across.

Row 2: P across.

Repeat rows 1 and 2.

Advanced Beginner

NOTES

• Do not join. Work back and forth on circular needle.

• Make sure to hold onto the two strands of eyelash yarn. They can slip easily.

• For a feathery effect, pull eyelash fibers out gently on ruffle.

• You can substitute any eyelash yarn for the ruffle in the same gauge.

Ruffle

Begin with 180" (6.4m) of cast on yarn. With US #10 circular needles working 1strand of Montage, 1 strand Sevilla and 2 strands of Perla, CO 221 sts.

Row 1: Knit across, do not connect row. Work knitting back and forth on needles to form straight knitting.

Row 2: K across.

Row 3: Drop Perla. Cont with 1 strand Montage and 1 strand Sevilla held tog, *K13, K2tog, K2tog. Repeat from * across = 195 sts.

Row 4: P across.

Row 5: *K11, K2tog, K2tog. Repeat from * across = 169 sts.

Row 6: P across.

Row 7: *K9, K2tog, K2tog. Repeat from * across = 143 sts.

Row 8: P across.

Row 9: *K7, K2tog, K2tog. Repeat from * across = 117 sts.

Row 10: P across.

Row 11: *K5, K2tog, K2tog. Repeat from * across = 91 sts.

Row 12: P across.

Row 13: *K3, K2tog, K2tog. Repeat from * across = 65 sts.

Row 14: P across.

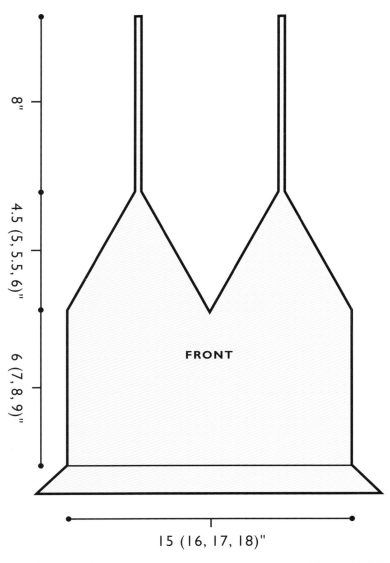

8"

4.5 (5, 5.5, 6)"

6 (7, 8, 9)"

FRONT

15 (16, 17, 18)"

Front

Next Row: Dec 5 (dec 1, inc 3, inc 7) sts evenly across the row. For all other sizes, inc 1 (3, 7) sts evenly across the row = 60 (64, 68, 72) sts. Change to US #10 straight needles. Work St st for 6 (7, 8, 9)"/15 (18, 20, 23)cm. Knit 30 (32, 34, 36) sts. Place rem sts on stitch holder. Work (RS) only: K2, Sl1, K1, PSSO (armhole side) work to last 4 sts from end, K2tog, K2, (neck edge). (WS) P across. Repeat last 2 rows and cont to dec K rows until 4 sts rem. Work even until strap measures 8" (20cm) or desired length. BO.

Place sts from holder onto needle. Repeat as for other side.

Finishing

Glue or sew 6 pink rosettes to front evenly spaced. Glue or sew large rosette to center of neckline. Sew four satin ribbon strands to both sides of halter back. Trim ends on an angle.

Round Capelet

Worked in the round, this vibrant wrap is knit with colorful twisted slubbed wool and accented with a soft fur edging. Take the hassle out of shaping with a simple knit-two stitches together decreasing technique. Ideal for a special school trip or that afternoon shopping spree with friends.

Yarn

2 (2,3,3) skeins *Schaefer Yarns* Elaine *300yds (277m) / 8oz (99% merino wool, 1% nylon) Color: Piggy*

2 (2,3,3) balls *Lion Brand Yarn* Fun Fur *64yds (59m) / 50g (100% polyester) Color: #100 White*

Needles

One pair each of US #17 (12.75mm) 36" (90cm) and US #13 (9mm) 16" (40cm) circular needles or size needed to obtain gauge.

Sizes

2–4, (6–8) yrs of age. Instructions are for smallest size, with changes for other sizes in parentheses.

Finished Measurements

Measures 24 (28)"/61 (71)cm wide x 14 (18)"/35.5 (45.5)cm long.

Gauge

In Stockinette Stitch Pattern, 12 sts and 12 rows = 4" (10cm) with US #15 (10mm) needles and 2 strands of Elaine yarn held tog.

Stockinette Stitch Pattern

Knit every round.

Advanced Beginner

NOTES

• After casting on, straighten stitches on circular needle before joining the row.

• Knitting every round with circular needles will produce a Stockinette Stitch Pattern.

• Comb fur fibers out gently along edging to fluff up.

• Do not block edging.

• You can substitute any long fur yarn for the edging in the same gauge.

Front and Back (one piece)

With US #15 circular needles working 1 strand of Elaine and 4 strands of fur yarn held tog, CO 143 (169) sts. Place a ring marker to note beginning of row.

Rnd 1: K

Rnd 2: P

Rnd 3: K

Rnd 4: Drop strands of fur yarn and add 1 strand of Elaine yarn. K rnd with 2 strands of Elaine held tog.

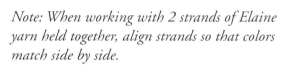

Note: When working with 2 strands of Elaine yarn held together, align strands so that colors match side by side.

Rnd 5: *K2tog, K2tog, K9. Repeat from * across = 121 (143) sts.

Rnds 6–17: K

Rnd 18: *K2tog, K2tog, K7. Repeat from * across = 99 (117) sts.

Rnds 19–30: K

Rnd 31: *K2tog, K2tog, K5. Repeat from * across = 77 (91) sts.

Rnds 32–40 : K

Rnd 41: *K2tog, K2tog, K3. Repeat from * across = 55 (65) sts.

Neckline

K even for 2 (5, 11, 11) rnds.

Next Rnd: Change to US #13 circular needles, and K 1 rnd.

Next Rnd: P

BO loosely.

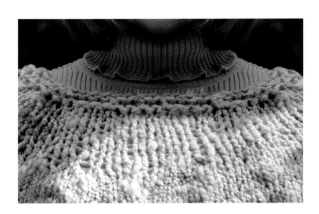

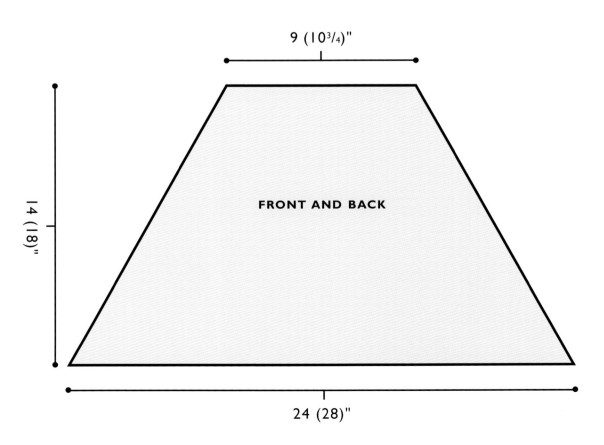

9 (10¾)"

14 (18)"

FRONT AND BACK

24 (28)"

Fuzzy Jacket

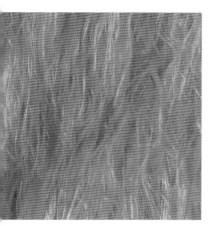

Young girls love pink! We searched for the most brilliant pink yarn to create this buttonless fuzzy jacket. It's worked in a Stockinette Stitch Pattern with a cotton base yarn, and blended with a soft fur yarn to create a furry texture. Simple shaping and straight sleeves create a seamless drop-sleeve style. Cool and sassy!

Yarn

1 (2,2,3) skeins *Colinette* SilkyChic *221yds (204m) / 100g (100% polyamide) Color: #140 Rio*

4 (4,5,5) skeins *Plassard* Mayotte *99yds (91m) / 50g (100% cotton) Color: #272*

Needles

US #9 (5.5mm) needles or size needed to obtain gauge.

Size I crochet hook.

Sizes

2 (4, 6, 8) yrs of age. Instructions are for smallest size, with changes for other sizes in parentheses.

Finished Measurements

Chest: 28 (29, 31, 33)"/71 (74, 79, 84)cm.

Total Length: 12.5 (13.5, 14.5, 15)"/32 (34, 37, 38)cm.

Gauge

In Stockinette Stitch Pattern, 13 sts and 20 rows = 4" (10cm) with 1 strand each of SilkyChic and Mayotte held tog.

Stockinette Stitch Pattern

Row 1: K across.
Row 2: P across.
Repeat rows 1 and 2.

Advanced Beginner

NOTES

- Comb fibers out gently along needle on each row.
- Make sure to hold onto the two strands. SilkyChic can slip easily.
- After assembly, comb out gently for fluffy effect.
- Fluff up in dryer on air cycle for 3 minutes before wearing.
- Do not block.
- You can substitute any twisted cotton yarn to pair with the SilkyChic for the jacket in the same gauge.

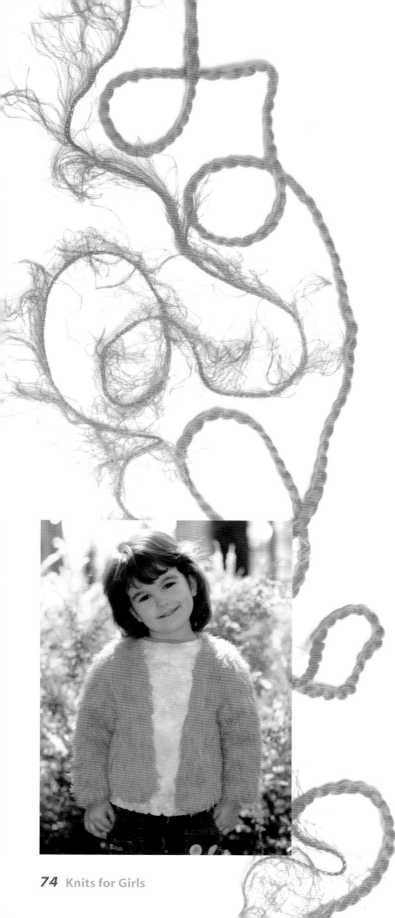

Back

Working 2 strands of SilkyChic and 1 strand of Mayotte held tog, CO 41 (44, 47, 50) sts. Work in Garter Stitch Pattern for 2 rows. Work the next 4 rows in Stockinette Stitch Pattern. Next row, drop 1 strand SilkyChic and cont with 1 strand of Mayotte, inc 4 sts across the first row, for a total of 45 (48, 51, 54) sts. Cont in St st until piece measures 12.5 (13.5, 14.5, 15)"/32 (34, 37, 38)cm. BO.

Left Front

Working 2 strands of SilkyChic and 1 strand of Mayotte held tog, CO 16 (19, 22, 25) sts. Work in Garter Stitch for 2 rows. Work the next 4 rows in St st. Next row, drop 1 strand SilkyChic and cont with 1 strand of Mayotte, inc 3 sts across the first row, for a total of 19 (22, 25, 28) sts. Cont in St st until piece measures 5 (6, 6.5, 7)"/12.5 (15, 16.5, 18)cm

Left Neck Shaping: BO 2 (2, 3, 3) sts at neck edge. Dec 1 st at neck edge every right side row 4 (4, 4, 4) times. 13 (16, 18, 21) sts remain. Cont until piece measures same as back and BO all sts.

Right Front

Work same as left front reversing shaping.

Sleeves

Working 2 strands of SilkyChic and 1 strand of Mayotte held tog, CO 16 (19, 22, 25) sts. Work in Garter Stitch Pattern for 2 rows. Work the next 4 rows in St st. Next row, drop 1 strand SilkyChic and cont with 1 strand of Mayotte, inc 2 (3, 4, 5) sts across the first row = 18 (22, 26, 30) sts. Inc 1 st each side every other row 4 (4, 4, 4) times, then every 4th row 5 (6, 7, 7) times to 36 (42, 48, 52) sts. Work even until sleeve measures 8 (9, 9.5, 10)"/20.5 (23, 24, 25.5)cm or desired length. BO.

Finishing

Sew shoulder seams. Sew sleeves into armholes. Sew sleeve and side seams. With I crochet hook, beginning at lower right front edge, crochet one row of single crochet around right front, neckline, and down left front.

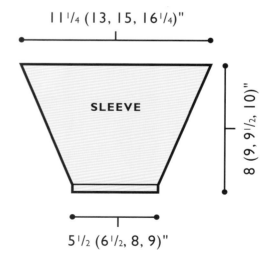

BACK

12¹⁄₂ (13¹⁄₂, 14¹⁄₂, 15)"

14 (14¹⁄₂, 15¹⁄₂, 16¹⁄₂)"

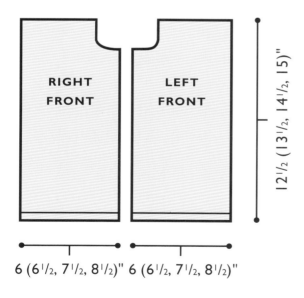

RIGHT FRONT

LEFT FRONT

12¹⁄₂ (13¹⁄₂, 14¹⁄₂, 15)"

6 (6¹⁄₂, 7¹⁄₂, 8¹⁄₂)" 6 (6¹⁄₂, 7¹⁄₂, 8¹⁄₂)"

11¹⁄₄ (13, 15, 16¹⁄₄)"

SLEEVE

8 (9, 9¹⁄₂, 10)"

5¹⁄₂ (6¹⁄₂, 8, 9)"

4 KNITS FOR BOYS

This chapter presents some fun projects for your little guy. The first project is a whimsical Snake Scarf guaranteed to grab his attention. Worked with fur and squiggly yarns on giant needles, this plush warm scarf doubles as a fuzzy animal friend. In the two-toned, chenille Cozy Scarf, he'll look cool but feel warm. The Wool Cap uses a chunky slubbed wool yarn for added warmth. The Handsome Vest is accented with a chunky ribbon yarn in an easy Stockinette Stitch Pattern. Puppet Mittens are sure to bring hours of fun and warmth on those cold afternoons at the playground. He'll have that all-grown-up look sporting the attractive, funnel-neck Easy Pullover worked in a soft synthetic blend.

The rugged Suede Sweater uses a synthetic yarn that feels like real soft suede. The Little Man Cardigan says it all. Knit in a wool and acrylic blend for plenty of warmth, this simple pattern makes it as much fun to knit as it is to wear.

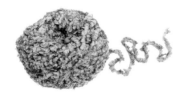

Snake Scarf

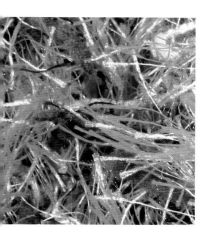

This fun scarf uses the Garter Stitch Pattern worked with Fur and Funky yarns. Use big needles for a quick finish. To create the puffy snake body, knit a long flat scarf and roll it into a boa. Finish the face with craft eyes, a button nose, and red felt tongue. This warm, cuddly scarf doubles as a plush animal friend!

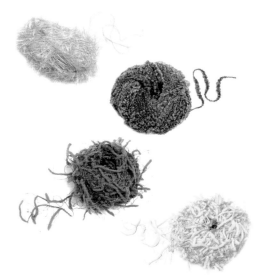

Yarn

1 ball *Gedifra* Astrakan *54yds (50m) / 50g (57% polyacryl, 43% wool) Color: #4706*

1 ball each *Crystal Palace Yarns* Squiggle *100yds (92m) / 50g (50% polyester, 50% nylon) Colors: #2264 Royal Purple and #4705 Pippin Green*

1 ball *Lion Brand Yarn* Fun Fur *60yds (55m) / 50g (100% polyester) Color: #105 Light Blue*

Needles

One pair each of US #11 (8mm) and US #19 (15mm) needles or size needed to obtain gauge.

Materials

2 Darice (24mm) animal eyes

1 double eye button

1 strip of red felt

Finished Measurements

Measures 12" (30.5cm) wide x 35" (101.5cm) long.

Gauge

In Garter Stitch Pattern, 13 sts and 20 rows = 4" (10cm) with Astrakan on smaller needles.

Garter Stitch Pattern

Knit every row.

Easy

NOTES

- For a thicker snake body, line flat knitting with polyester fiberfill before rolling into boa shape.
- For fluffy effect, pull fibers out gently.
- You can substitute any fur or bouclé yarn in the same gauge.

Head

With US #11 needles and Astrakan, CO 4 sts. Inc one st at the beg and end of each row for 18 rows = 40 sts. Knit 2 rows even.

Body

Drop Astrakan. Change to US #19 needles. Working 1 strand each Fun Fur, Squiggle Royal Purple and Squiggle Pippin Green held tog, K for 30" (76cm) or desired length.

K2tog across row = 20 sts remain.

K2tog across row = 10 sts remain.

Tail

Drop Fun Fur and Squiggle yarns and add Astrakan. K2tog across row. 5 sts remain.

Knit for 5" (12.5cm). K2tog, K, K2tog. BO last 3 sts.

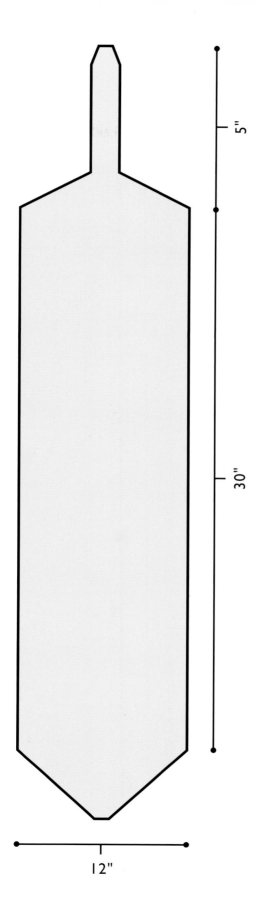

5"

30"

12"

Finishing

Straighten and lay flat. Position eyes and snap into place. Roll width into a cylindrical boa shape, forming a point for the nose. With Fun Fur yarn and tapestry needle, sew long edges together. Sew nose button. Cut tongue from red felt and sew into snake's mouth.

Cozy Scarf

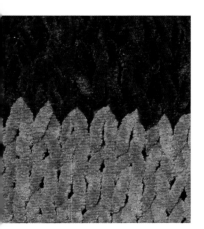

Keep your little guy warm with this handsome scarf, worked in a faux suede chenille yarn. The pattern uses rich Mocha and Coffee colors in each half of the scarf, creating a 2-inch band along the bottom. Knit the pattern in a short or long version, fold, and sew side seams together. Finish with short fringe along the bottom edges. A perfect two-toned combination!

Yarn

1 (1,2,2) skeins *Lion Brand Yarn* Lion Suede *122yds (110m) / 85g (100% polyester) Color: #126 Coffee*

1 (1,2,2) skeins *Lion Brand Yarn* Lion Suede *122yds (110m) / 85g (100% polyester) Color: #125 Mocha*

Needles

US #13 (9mm) needles or size needed to obtain gauge.

Size I crochet hook.

Sizes

2–4 (6–8) yrs of age. Instructions are for shortest size, with changes for other sizes in parentheses.

Finished Measurements

Measures 3.25 (6.5)"/8 (16.5)cm wide x 30 (60)"/76 (1.5)m long when folded.

Gauge

In Stockinette Stitch Pattern, 11 sts and 12 rows = 4" (10cm).

Stockinette Stitch Pattern

Row 1: K across.
Row 2: P across.
Repeat rows 1 and 2.

Beginner

NOTES

- Keep tension loose, as yarn does not stretch.
- You can substitute any faux suede yarn for the scarf in the same gauge.

Body

Working 1 strand of Mocha, CO 18 (36) sts.

Rows 1 & 2: K across.

Row 3: P across.

Row 4: K across.

Row 5: P across.

Row 6: K across.

Row 7: Drop Mocha, add Coffee and P across.

Work in St st for 15 (30)"/38 (76)cm or desired length.

Drop Coffee, add Mocha. Work St st for 15 (30)"/38 (75)cm or make even with other side ending with a P row.

Next row: Drop Mocha, add Coffee and K across.

Next row: P across.

Next row: K across.

Next row: P across.

Next row: K across.

Next row: P across.

K last 2 rows. BO loosely.

Finishing

Lay scarf straight and flat. Fold in half vertically. Align edges and sew with monofilament thread along seam.

Do not sew bottom ends.

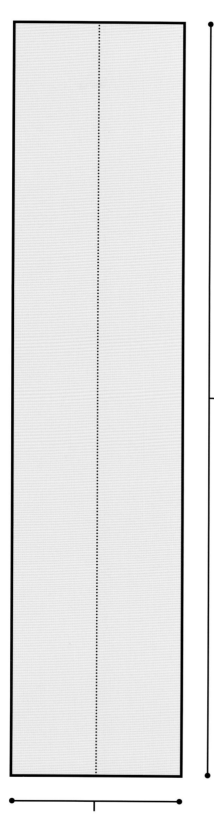

30 (60)"

6¹/₂ (13)"

Fringe

For the Coffee bottom edge, cut Mocha yarn into 6" (15cm) lengths. Fold in half and loop all the way through two layers of the first stitch with size I crochet hook. Repeat equally along the edge.

For the Mocha bottom edge, cut Coffee yarn into 6" (15cm) lengths. Fold in half and loop all the way through two layers of the first stitch with size I crochet hook. Repeat equally along the edge.

Trim fringe evenly to 2.5" (6cm).

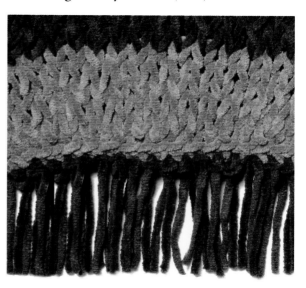

Wool Cap

This great-looking cap combines two thick wool yarns to create a layered texture that has both volume and warmth. The bulky band is worked in a wool blend, while the slubbed variegated yarn makes up the body. This sturdy, earth-tone cap is an ideal accessory for chilly days.

Yarn
1 skein *Plymouth Yarn* Encore Chunky *143yds (132m) / 100g (75% acrylic, 25% wool) Color: #1444*

1 ball *Plassard* Versatile *54yds (50m) / 50g (100% wool) Color: 004*

Needles
US #13 (9mm) 16" (40cm) circular needles or size needed to obtain gauge.

Sizes
One size fits all.

Finished Measurements
Measures 8" (20cm) wide x 7" (18cm) long.

Gauge
In Stockinette Stitch Pattern, 14 sts and 16 rows = 4" (10cm) with Versatile yarn.

Stockinette Stitch Pattern
Knit every round.

Beginner

NOTES
- You can substitute any slubbed yarn for Versatile in the same gauge.
- You can substitute any worsted weight for Encore yarn in the same gauge.

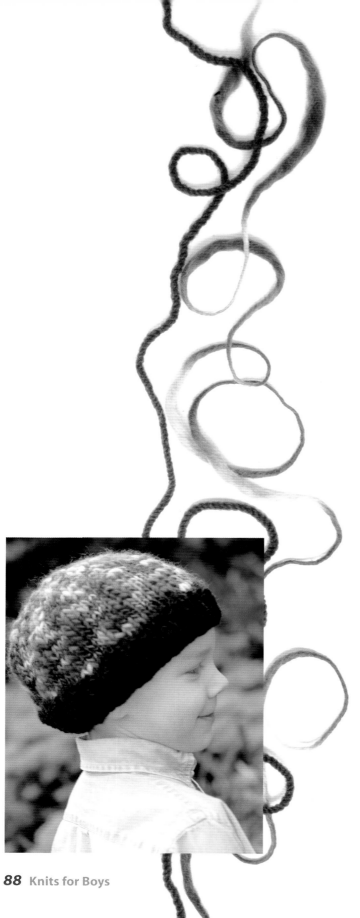

Front and Back

Working 1 strand of Encore, CO 60 sts.

Rnd 1: (RS) *K2, P2. Repeat from * across.

Rnd 2: *P2, K2. Repeat from * across.

Rnd 3: *K2, P2. Repeat from * across.

Rnd 4: *P2, K2. Repeat from * across.

Rnd 5: *K2, P2. Repeat from * across.

Rnd 6: *P2, K2. Repeat from * across.

Rnd 7: *K2, P2. Repeat from * across.

Rnds 8–18: Change to 1 strand of Versatile and knit across.

Rnd 19: K8, K2 tog. Repeat from * across.

Rnd 20: K across.

Rnd 21: *K7, K2 tog. Repeat from * across.

Rnd 22: K across.

Rnd 23: *K6, K2 tog. Repeat from * across.

Rnd 24: K across.

Rnd 25: *K5, K2 tog. Repeat from * across.

Rnd 26: K across.

Rnd 27: *K4, K2 tog. Repeat from * across.

Rnd 28: *K3, K2 tog. Repeat from * across.

Rnd 29: *K2, K2 tog. Repeat from * across.

Rnd 30: K2 tog across = 9 sts.

Finishing

Cut yarn, thread through a tapestry needle, and work through rem 9 sts. Pull tightly to close and fasten off.

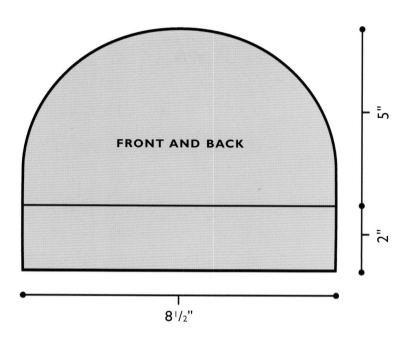

FRONT AND BACK

5"

2"

8 ¹/₂"

Color Variation

Knit as pattern above. Substitute Encore *Color: #1444* for Encore *Color: #217.* Substitute Versatile *Color: #004* for Versatile *Color: #002.*

Handsome Vest

This attractive little boy's vest features a simple Stockinette Stitch Pattern. The red color band in front and back is created from a mix of Ribbon chenille and bouclé yarns. Chunky ribbing gives this vest the perfect plush feel. An easy-to-knit and assemble beginner project guaranteed to build your knitting confidence.

Yarn

1 (1,1,2) skeins *Plymouth Yarn* Encore *143yds (132m) / 100g (75% acrylic, 25% wool) Color: #599*

3 (3,4,4) balls *Lana Grossa* Favola *65yds (60m) / 50g (40% wool, 30% polyamide, 30% acrylic) Color: #12*

1 (1,2,2) balls *Filatura di Crosa* Ananas *55yds (50m) / 50g (65% viscose, 15% acrylic, 20% polyamide) Color: #103*

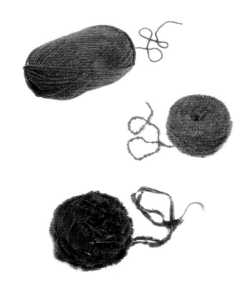

Needles

One pair each of US #10.5 (6.5mm), US #11 (8mm) and US #13 (9mm) needles or size needed to obtain gauge.

Size J crochet hook.

Sizes

2 (4, 6, 8) yrs of age. Instructions are for smallest size, with changes for other sizes in parentheses.

Finished Measurements

Chest: 25 (28, 32, 36)"/64 (71, 81, 91)cm.

Total Length: 12 .75 (15, 17.25, 18.25)"/32 (38, 44, 46.5) cm.

Gauge

In Stockinette Stitch Pattern, 9 sts and 16 rows = 4" (10cm) with 1 strand of Encore and Liberty held tog.

Stockinette Stitch Pattern

Row 1: K across.
Row 2: P across.
Repeat rows 1 and 2.

Beginner

NOTES

- Make sure to hold onto the two strands of yarn, they can slip easily.
- You can substitute Liberty yarn for Favola yarn.

2x2 Ribbing Pattern

Row 1: (WS) *P2, K2; Repeat from * to end of row.

Row 2: *K2, P2; Repeat from * to end of row. Repeat rows 1 and 2.

Back

With US #10.5 needles and 2 strands of Encore held tog, CO 33 (37, 41, 45) sts.

Row 1: (WS) P1, *K2, P2 repeat from * to end.

Row 2: (RS) K2, *P2, K2 repeat from * to end.

Work ribbing for 7 (7, 9, 9) rows, ending with row 1.

Next row: (RS) Change to US #13 needles. Drop 1 strand of Encore and add 1 strand Liberty. Work in St st, dec 5 sts evenly across the 1st row 28 (32, 36, 40) sts. Work even for 2.5 (3, 3.5, 4)"/6 (8, 9,10)cm.

For the color band, change to US #11 needles, drop 1 strand Encore, and add 1 strand Ananas. Cont St st for 3 (3.25, 3.5, 4)"/7.5 (8, 9, 10)cm.

Armhole Shaping

Return to US #13 needles. Drop Ananas and add one strand Liberty and BO 2 sts at the beg of the next 2 rows = 24 (28, 32, 36) sts. Dec 1 st at each armhole edge 2 times = 20 (24, 28, 32) sts. Cont until armhole measures 5.5 (7, 8, 8)"/14 (18, 20.5, 20.5)cm. BO loosely.

Front

Work same as back until armhole shaping is completed.

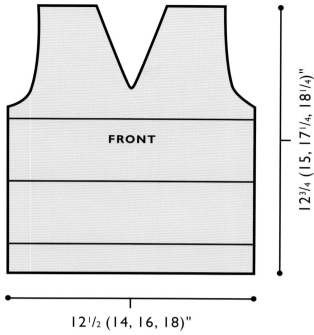

FRONT

12³/₄ (15, 17¹/₄, 18¹/₄)"

12¹/₂ (14, 16, 18)"

BACK

12³/₄ (15, 17¹/₄, 18¹/₄)"

12¹/₂ (14, 16, 18)"

Neck Shaping

With 20 (24, 28, 32) sts, work 10 (12, 14, 16) sts and place rem sts on stitch holder. P back across on needle.

Dec 1 st at neck edge as foll: Work to last 3 sts (K2tog, K1) 4 times = 6 (8, 10, 12) sts.

When armhole measures same as back, BO 6 (8, 10, 12) sts for shoulder. Work other neck shaping, dec by K1, SL1, K1 PSSO at neck edge.

Finishing

Sew side seams. With size J crochet hook, single crochet around neck and armhole edges with Encore and Liberty.

Color Variation

Knit as pattern above. Substitute Liberty *Color: #7* for Favola *Color: #12*. Substitute Ananas *Color: #103* for Ananas *Color: #113*. Substitute Encore *Color: #599* for Encore *Color: #217*.

Puppet Mittens

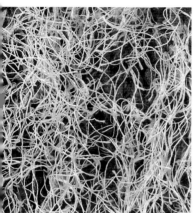

Kids will take care not to lose these playful mittens which are knit in one piece using warm wool-blend and Fur yarns in Ribbing and Stockinette Stitch Patterns. Attach big eyes, fold and sew side seams to form pockets for fingers and thumb. Mix and match colors for fun!

Yarn
1 (1,1,1) skein *Plymouth Yarn* Encore *200yds (185m) / 100g (75% acrylic, 25% wool) Color: #1384*

1 (1,1,1) ball *Crystal Palace Yarns* Fizz *120yds (110m) / 50g (100% polyester) Color: #9224 Lime Green*

Needles
US #10 (6mm) needles or size needed to obtain gauge.

Materials
2 Darice (24mm) comical eyes

Sizes
2–6 yrs of age. Instructions are for all sizes.

Finished Measurements
Measures 7.5"/19cm wide x 3"/8cm long when folded.

Gauge
In Stockinette Stitch Pattern, 16 sts and 22 rows = 4" (10cm).

Stockinette Stitch Pattern
Row 1: K across.
Row 2: P across.
Repeat rows 1 and 2.

2x2 Ribbing Pattern
Row 1: (RS) *K2, P2; Repeat from * to end of row.
Row 2: *P2, K2; Repeat from * to end of row.
Repeat rows 1 and 2.

Beginner

NOTES
• Pull fibers out gently for fluffy effect.
• You can substitute any worsted weight yarn in the same gauge.

Body (make two)

Working 2 strands of Encore #1384 held tog, CO 12 sts.

Rows 1–12: Work 2x2 Ribbing for 12 rows.

Rows 13–33: Add 1 strand of Fizz Lime Green and work St st for 20 rows.

Row 34: (RS) K2tog, K across, K2tog.

Row 35: P across.

Row 36: K2tog, K2tog, K across, K2tog, K2tog.

Row 37: P across.

Row 38: K2tog, K across, K2tog. (4 sts rem)

Row 39: Drop Fizz. P across.

Row 40: Inc 1, K across, inc 1.

Row 41: P across.

Row 42: Inc 1, inc 1, K across, inc 1, inc 1.

Row 43: P across.

Row 44: Inc 1, K across, inc 1.

Row 45: P across.

Rows 46–84: K across.

Row 85: K2tog, K across, K2tog.

Row 86: P across.

Row 87: K2tog, K2tog, K across, K2tog, K2tog.

Row 88: P across.

Row 89: K2tog, K across, K2tog. (4 sts rem)

Row 90: P across.

Row 91: Add 1 strand of Fizz Lime Green and inc 1, K across, inc 1.

Row 92: P across.

Row 93: Inc 1, inc 1, K across, inc 1, inc 1.

Row 94: P across.

Row 95: Inc 1, K across, inc 1.

Row 96: P across.

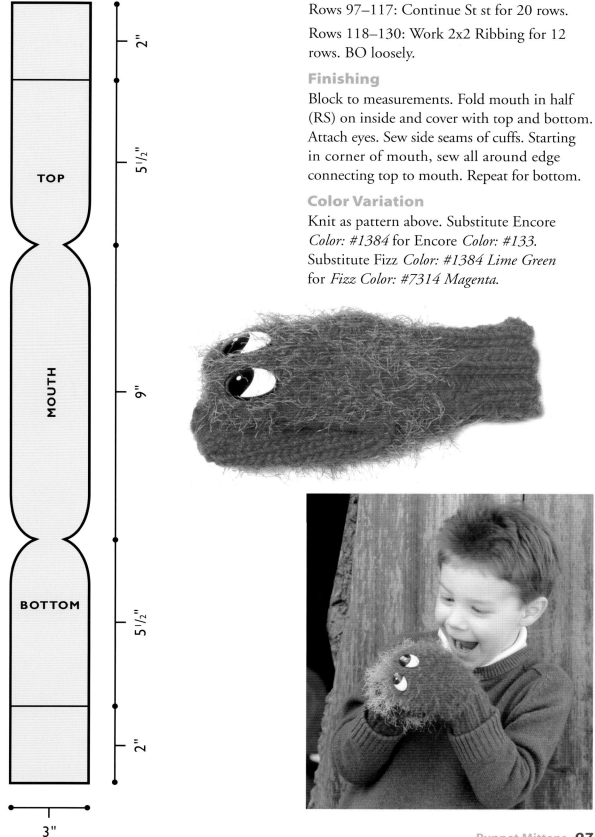

Rows 97–117: Continue St st for 20 rows.

Rows 118–130: Work 2x2 Ribbing for 12 rows. BO loosely.

Finishing

Block to measurements. Fold mouth in half (RS) on inside and cover with top and bottom. Attach eyes. Sew side seams of cuffs. Starting in corner of mouth, sew all around edge connecting top to mouth. Repeat for bottom.

Color Variation

Knit as pattern above. Substitute Encore *Color: #1384* for Encore *Color: #133*. Substitute Fizz *Color: #1384 Lime Green* for *Fizz Color: #7314 Magenta*.

2"

5½"

TOP

MOUTH

9"

BOTTOM

5½"

2"

3"

Easy Pullover

This handsome pullover features a roomy funnel neck for comfort and a stylish look. The sweater is worked in soft nylon in a simple Stockinette Stitch Pattern. This super easy top has the feel of soft cashmere and is accented with a soft wool blend for the cuffs and waistband. Boys will love it!

Yarn

5 (5,6,6) balls *Crystal Palace Yarns* Poof *47yds (43m) / 50g (100% nylon) Color: #3609*

1 (1,1,1) ball *Gedifra* Fashion Trend *98yds (90m) / 50g (51% wool, 49% acrylic) Color: #4502*

Needles

One pair each of US #10 (6mm) and US #11 (8mm) needles or size needed to obtain gauge.

Sizes

2 (4, 6, 8) yrs of age. Instructions are for smallest size, with changes for other sizes in parentheses.

Finished Measurements

Chest: 26 (28, 30, 32)"/66 (71, 76, 81)cm.

Total Length: 13 (14, 15, 16)"/33 (35.5, 38, 40.5)cm.

Gauge

In Stockinette Stitch Pattern, 8 sts and 13 rows = 4" (10cm) with US #11 needles and Poof yarn.

Garter Stitch Pattern

Knit every row.

Stockinette Stitch Pattern

Row 1: K across.
Row 2: P across.
Repeat rows 1 and 2.

Beginner

NOTES

- Keep tension loose, as the yarn does not stretch.
- You can substitute any wool blend yarn for the waistband or cuffs in the same gauge.

Back

With US #10 needles and Fashion Trend yarn, CO 36 (38, 40, 42) sts. Work in Garter Stitch pattern for 10 rows. Change to US #11 needles and Poof yarn. Working in St st, dec 10 sts evenly across 1st row = 26 (28, 30, 32) sts. Work even until piece measures 13 (14, 15, 16)"/33 (35.5, 38, 40.5)cm.

Next row: BO 6 (7, 7, 8) sts. Work 14 (14, 16, 16) sts. BO last 6 (7, 7, 8) sts.

Reattach yarn at neck edge. Work 3 (5, 5, 5) rows. BO loosely.

Front

Work same as back.

Sleeves

With US #10 needles and Fashion Trend yarn, CO 18 (20, 22, 24) sts. Work 10 rows in Garter Stitch Pattern. Change to US #11 needles and Poof yarn. Working in St st, dec 6 (7, 8, 9) sts evenly across 1st row = 12 (13, 14, 15) sts. Inc 1 st each end every 4th row 2 (5, 2, 3) times every 6th row 3 (1, 4, 4) times = 22 (25, 26, 29) sts. Work even until sleeve measures 10.5 (10.5, 12.5, 13)"/26.5 (26.5, 32, 33)cm or desired length. BO loosely.

Finishing

Sew shoulder and neck seams together. Sew in sleeve. Sew sleeve and underarm seams together.

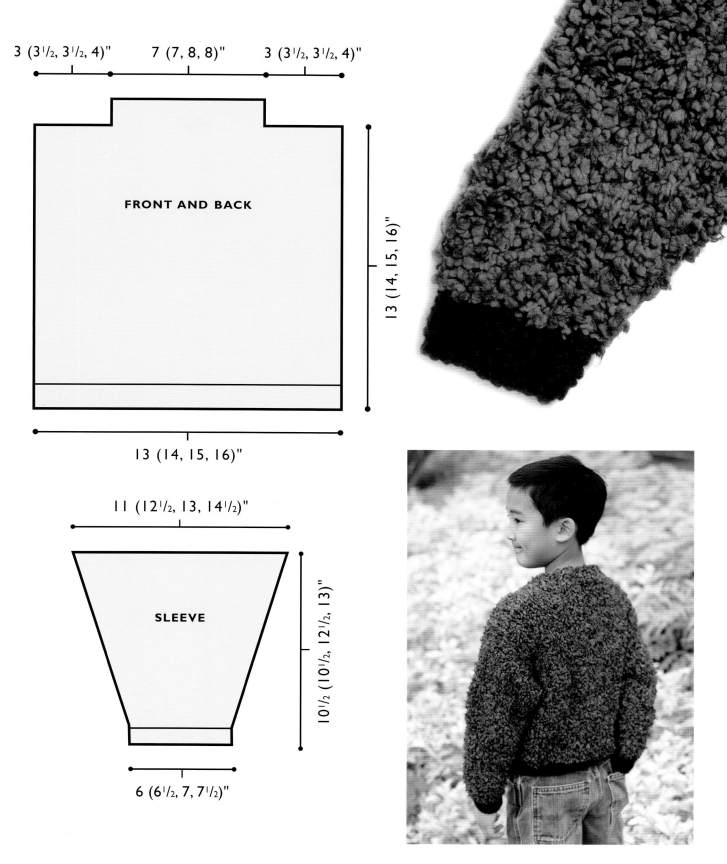

3 (3¹/₂, 3¹/₂, 4)"   7 (7, 8, 8)"   3 (3¹/₂, 3¹/₂, 4)"

FRONT AND BACK

13 (14, 15, 16)"

13 (14, 15, 16)"

11 (12¹/₂, 13, 14¹/₂)"

SLEEVE

10¹/₂ (10¹/₂, 12¹/₂, 13)"

6 (6¹/₂, 7, 7¹/₂)"

Suede Sweater

This classic boat neck sweater worked in green and beige faux suede yarns is great for every occasion. Straight knitting for the front and back pieces and minimal shaping for the sleeves makes this a great beginner sweater project. Single ribbing accents the cuffs and waistband, and provides both resiliency and handsome styling.

Yarn

3 (4,4,4) skeins *Berroco* Suede *120yds (111m) / 50g (100% nylon) Color: #3714*

3 (4,4,4) skeins *Berroco* Suede *120yds (111m) / 50g (100% nylon) Color: #3716*

1 (2,2,2) skeins *Berroco* Denim Silk *105yds (97m) / 50g (20% silk, 80% rayon) Color: #1405*

Needles

US #10 (6mm) needles or size needed to obtain gauge.

Sizes

2 (4, 6, 8) yrs of age. Instructions are for smallest size, with changes for other sizes in parentheses.

Finished Measurements

Chest: 26 (28, 30, 32)"/66 (71, 76, 81)cm.

Total Length: 15 (16, 17, 18)"/38 (40.5, 43, 45.5)cm.

Gauge

In Stockinette Stitch Pattern, 16 sts and 20 rows = 4" (10cm).

Stockinette Stitch Pattern

Row 1: K across.
Row 2: P across.
Repeat rows 1 and 2.

Beginner

NOTES

• Keep tension loose, as the suede yarn does not stretch.
• You can substitute any faux suede yarn for the sweater in the same gauge.

Single Ribbing

Row 1: (WS) *P1, K1; Repeat from * to end of row.

Row 2: *K1, P1; Repeat from * to end of row. Repeat rows 1 and 2.

Back

With US #10 needles and 2 strands of DenimSilk yarn held tog, CO 52 (56, 60, 64) sts. Work in Single Ribbing for 1.5" (4cm).

Change to 1 strand each of Suede #3716 and #3714 and work in St st until work measures 15 (16, 17, 18)"/38 (40.5, 43, 45.5)cm from beginning. BO loosely.

Front

Work same as for back.

Sleeves

With US #10 needles and 2 strands of DenimSilk yarn held tog, CO 24 (30, 34, 38) sts. Work in Single Ribbing for 1.5" (4cm).

Change to 1 strand each of Suede #3716 and #3714 and inc 1 st each side every 4th row 11 times. Work even on 46 (52, 56, 60) sts until sleeve measures 10.5 (11, 12, 13)"/26.5 (28, 30.5, 33)cm. BO loosely.

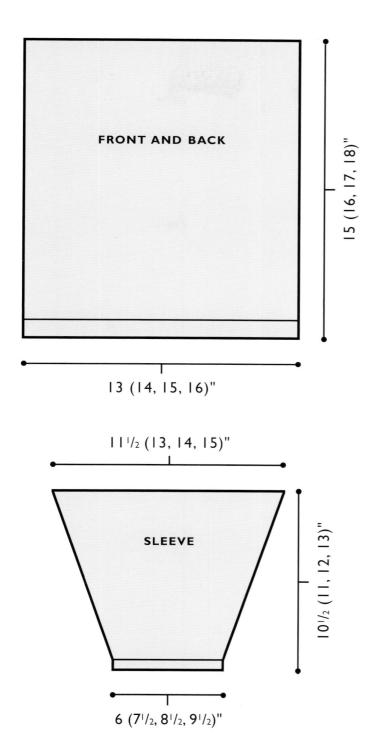

FRONT AND BACK

15 (16, 17, 18)"

13 (14, 15, 16)"

11½ (13, 14, 15)"

SLEEVE

10½ (11, 12, 13)"

6 (7½, 8½, 9½)"

Finishing
To form boat neck, sew front and back shoulder seams together 3 (3.5, 3.5, 3.5)"/7.5 (9, 9, 9)cm from each end. Mark armhole openings for sleeves. Sew sleeves into armholes. Sew side and sleeve seams.

Little Man Cardigan

This cardigan is worked in an easy Stockinette Stitch Pattern on 10.5 needles. The wool-and-acrylic-blend yarn provides plenty of warmth and is durable enough for outdoor play. Accented with four large buttons and ribbed on the sleeves and waistband, every little boy is guaranteed to look all grown up.

Yarn

2 (2,3,3) balls *Berroco* Softwist Bulky *136yds (126m) / 100g (41% wool, 59% rayon) Color: #7479*

3 (4,4,5) balls *Berroco* Medley *73yds (67m) / 50g (75% wool, 15% acrylic, 10% nylon) Color: #8913*

Needles

One pair each of US #9 (5.5mm) and US #10.5 (6.5mm) needles or size needed to obtain gauge.

Size I crochet hook.

Materials

4 buttons 1" (2.5)cm in diameter

Sizes

2 (4, 6, 8) yrs of age. Instructions are for smallest size, with changes for other sizes in parentheses.

Finished Measurements

Chest: 24 (25, 26, 28)"/61 (64, 66, 71)cm.

Total Length: 14.5 (15.5, 16, 17.5)"/37 (39.5, 40.5, 44.5)cm.

Gauge

In Stockinette Stitch Pattern, 10 sts and 16 rows = 4" (10cm) with US #10.5 needles and 1 strand each Softwist and Medley held tog.

Stockinette Stitch Pattern

Row 1: K across.

Row 2: P across.

Repeat rows 1 and 2.

Advanced Beginner

NOTES

- Make sure to hold onto the two strands of yarn, they can easily slip.
- You can substitute any wool yarn for the ribbing in the same gauge.

2x2 Ribbing Pattern

Row 1: (RS) *K2, P2 repeat from * to end.

Row 2: K2, *P2, K2 repeat from * to end.

Repeat rows 1 and 2.

Back

With #9 needles and 2 strands Softwist held tog, CO 45 (45, 49, 49) sts. Work in ribbing for 7 (7, 9, 9) rows, ending with row 1.

Next row: (WS) Change to #10.5 needles and work 1 strand each of Softwist and Medley yarns held tog work in St st dec 15 (14, 16, 14) sts across the row = 30 (31, 33, 35) sts. Work even in St st until piece measures 14.5 (15.5, 16, 17.5)"/37 (39, 40.5, 44.5)cm. BO all sts.

Left Front

Work with #9 needles and 2 strands Softwist held tog, CO 25 (25, 29, 29) sts work in ribbing, except row 4.

Row 4: Work to 4 sts before the end, BO 2 to form buttonhole. Work last 2 sts.

Row 5: Work first 2 sts, CO 2 (buttonhole formed) work to end. Change to #10.5 needles and 1 strand each Medley and Soft Bulky yarns held tog and dec 9 (6, 9, 7) sts across 1st row = 16 (19, 20, 22) sts. Repeat 3 buttonholes evenly spaced between last buttonhole and first neck dec. When work measures 8.5 (9, 9.5,10)"/21.5 (23, 24, 25.5)cm, begin shaping neck as follows: Work to last 3 sts, K2 tog, K1, repeat this dec every (RS) row 8 (8, 9, 9) times = 8 (11, 11, 13) sts remaining. Work even until same length as back. BO loosely.

Right Front

Work same as left front, reversing shaping and omit buttonholes. Neck dec will be at the beginning of the row: K1, Sl1, K1 PSSO, K to end of row.

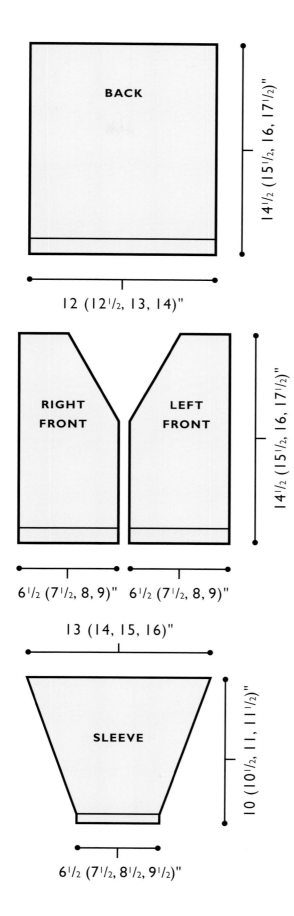

BACK

$14\frac{1}{2}$ ($15\frac{1}{2}$, 16, $17\frac{1}{2}$)"

12 ($12\frac{1}{2}$, 13, 14)"

RIGHT FRONT

LEFT FRONT

$14\frac{1}{2}$ ($15\frac{1}{2}$, 16, $17\frac{1}{2}$)"

$6\frac{1}{2}$ ($7\frac{1}{2}$, 8, 9)" $6\frac{1}{2}$ ($7\frac{1}{2}$, 8, 9)"

13 (14, 15, 16)"

SLEEVE

10 ($10\frac{1}{2}$, 11, $11\frac{1}{2}$)"

$6\frac{1}{2}$ ($7\frac{1}{2}$, $8\frac{1}{2}$, $9\frac{1}{2}$)"

Sleeves

Work with #9 needles and 2 strands Softwist held tog, CO 25 (25, 29, 29). Work in ribbing as for back. Next row: (WS) Change to #10.5 needles and work 1 strand each of Softwist and Medley yarns held tog work in St st and dec 9 (6, 8, 5) sts = 16 (19, 21, 24) sts. Inc 1 st each side every 4th row 8 (8, 8, 8) times = 32 (35, 37, 40) sts. Work until sleeve measures 10 (10.5, 11, 11.5)"/25 (27, 28, 29)cm, or desired length. BO loosely.

Finishing

Match up sides and sew shoulder seams together. Sew sleeves into place. Sew sleeves and side seams. With size I crochet hook, beginning at lower right front, single crochet in 2 out of every 3 sts around right front, neck, and left front. Sew on buttons.

5 KNITS FOR GIRLS AND BOYS

Pillows, blankets, and cushions are ideal for decorating a child's room, and make perfect gifts for any occasion.

The Fun Cushion tops are knit with bulky, multi-strand acrylic and wool-blend yarns that are soft to the touch but hold up well under daily use. Attach handmade tassels to each corner for a fun finishing touch.

The Party Pillows combine micro-fiber fur and long fur yarns to create a fuzzy, cozy fabric. The pillow patterns offer colorful variations. Try mixing and matching various yarn colors to add a decorative flair to your child's room.

The Cuddle Blanket is knit with bulky chenille yarn on a circular needle to accommodate a large number of stitches.

These fun decorative projects can spice up a room or create a cozy atmosphere.

Fun Cushions

Perfect for kids' rooms, these comfy cushion tops are versatile and fun. Super chunky, Multi-strand yarn is paired with a bulky wool-blend for a lush tactile texture. The knitted fabric is sewn onto store-bought giant denim pillows, finished with braided trim, and accented with handmade tassels.

Yarn

2 skeins *Skacel* Sofa *94yds (87m) / 200g (67% acrylic, 33% polyester) Color: #4802*

1 ball *Lion Brand Yarn* Wool-Ease Chunky *153yds (140m) / 140g (80% acrylic, 20% wool) Color: #112 Red*

See page 122 for yarn specifications for blue and lavender variations.

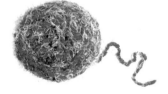

Needles

US #35 (19mm) needles or size needed to obtain gauge.

Materials

Denim decorator pillows 26" (66cm) wide x 26" (66cm) long

3yds (2.8m) each braided trim edging. *Colors: Red and Black*

Finished Measurements

Measures 26" (66cm) wide x 26" (66cm) long.

Gauge

In Stockinette Stitch Pattern 4 sts and 2.5 rows = 4" (10cm).

Stockinette Stitch Pattern

Row 1: K across.
Row 2: P across.
Repeat rows 1 and 2.

Easy

NOTES

• Take care to avoid splitting stitches when working with two strands of yarn.

• Make sure to hold onto the two strands of yarn, as they can easily slip.

• You can substitute any bulky yarn in the same gauge to combine with the Sofa yarn.

Cushion Top (one piece)

With #35 needles, working 1 strand of Sofa color #4802 and Wool-Ease color 112 Red held tog, CO 30 sts. Work Garter Stitch Pattern all rows for 26"/(66)cm or desired length. BO loosely.

Finishing

Sew braided trim around the edge of the pillow seam. Position knitted piece squarely atop pillow, sew cushion top to trim and through pillow along the perimeter of the seam.

Tassels

Make eight 4" (10cm) tassels (page 35) from Wool-Ease red. Attach one tassel to each corner of the cushion.

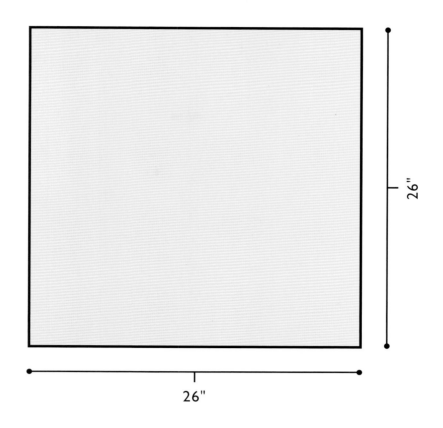

26"

26"

Color Variations

Blue

Knit as pattern above. Substitute Sofa *Color: #4802* for Sofa *Color: #4806.* Substitute Wool-Ease *Color: #112 Red* for Wool-Ease *Color: #109 Royal Blue.*

Lavender

Knit as pattern above. Substitute Sofa *Color: #4802* for Sofa *Color: #4793.* Substitute Wool-Ease *Color: #112 Red* for Wool-Ease *Color: #146 Orchid.*

Party Pillows

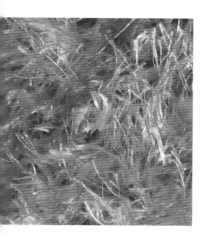

Cool for parties and decorating kids' rooms, these fab pillows are fuzzy and fun! Simply knit two squares, sew them together, and insert a pillow form. Feathery soft micro-fiber fur yarn is combined with long fur yarn for a furry fabric texture. Mix and match sides for a funky look! Soft and huggable, these puffy projects also make great gifts.

Yarn

2 balls *Crystal Palace Yarns* Splash *85yds (78m) / 100g (100% polyester) Color: #9219 Strawberry Soda*

2 balls *Lion Brand Yarn* Fun Fur *60yds (54m) / 50g (100% polyester) Color: #195 Hot Pink*

Needles

US #13 (9mm) needles or size needed to obtain gauge.

Materials

1 pillow form 14" (35.5cm) wide x 14" (35.5cm) long

Finished Measurements

Measures 14" (35.5cm) wide x 14" (35.5cm) long.

Gauge

In Garter Stitch Pattern, 11 sts and 14 rows = 4" (10cm).

Garter Stitch Pattern

Knit every row.

Easy

NOTES

- Take care to avoid splitting stitches when working with two strands of yarn.
- Make sure to hold onto the two strands of yarn, as they can slip easily.
- You can substitute any long fur yarn in the same gauge to combine with the Splash yarn.

Pillow (two pieces)

With US #13 needles, working 1 strand each of Splash Strawberry Soda and Fun Fur Hot Pink held tog, CO 39 sts. Work Garter Stitch Pattern all rows for 14"/(35.5)cm or desired length. BO loosely.

Finishing

With right sides facing, sew 3 sides, turn inside out. Slip in pillow form and sew side seam closed.

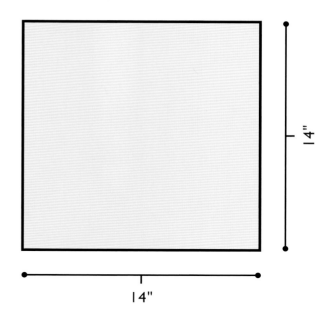

14"

14"

Color Variations

Orange

Knit as pattern above. Substitute Splash *Color: #9219 Strawberry Soda* for Splash *Color: #9216 Orangeade.* Substitute Fun Fur *Color: #195 Hot Pink* for Fun Fur *Color: #158 Bright Yellow.*

Lime

Knit as pattern above. Substitute Splash *Color: #9219 Strawberry Soda* for Splash *Color: #7232 Seafoam.* Substitute Fun Fur *Color: #195 Hot Pink* for Fun Fur *Color: #194 Lime.*

Cuddle Blanket

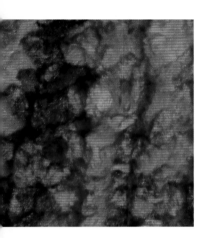

Super-soft and warm, this cuddly blanket is sure to be cherished by everyone in the family. It is knit with super bulky chenille yarn on large circular needles. An easy Garter Stitch Pattern makes this a fun project to knit. Great as a blanket, coverlet or throw. Ideal for curling up in front of the TV or a cozy park bench on a cool Fall day.

Yarn

3 skeins *Skacel* No Kidding *88yds (81m) / 200g (100% acryl)*
Color: #1138

Needles

US #17 (12mm) 36" (91cm) circular needles or size needed to obtain gauge.

Size K crochet hook.

Finished Measurements

Measures 36" (91cm) wide x 36" (91cm) long.

Gauge

In Garter Stitch Pattern, 6 sts and 8 rows = 4" (10cm).

Garter Stitch Pattern

Knit every row.

Beginner

- Knit loosely to keep stitches moving easily along the flexible cord and onto the needles.
- Do not join. Work back and forth on circular needle.
- Turn your work at the end of each row.

Blanket

With US #17 needles, CO 54 sts. Work back and forth in Garter Stitch Pattern all rows for 36"/(91)cm or desired length. BO loosely. Knit across, do not connect row.

Fringe

Cut yarn into 8" (20cm) lengths. Fold in half and loop through first stitch at end of blanket with a size K crochet hook. Repeat equally along the top and bottom edges every other stitch. Trim fringe evenly to 3" (7.5cm).

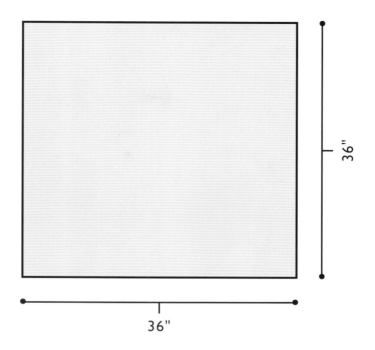

36"

36"

Skill Level Project Guide

Easy – Projects for first time knitters using basic knit stitches.

Beginner – Projects using basic Garter, or Stockinette Stitch Patterns with minimal shaping and assembly.

Candy Scarf 40

Jelly Flip-flops 44

Jelly Purse 48

Hawaiian Crop Top 52

Rainbow Poncho 56

Snake Scarf 78

Wrap Poncho 60

Cozy Scarf 82

Fun Cushions 112

Party Pillows 116

Wool Cap 86

Handsome Vest 90

Puppet Mittens
94

Easy Pullover 98

Suede Sweater
102

Cuddle Blanket
120

Advanced Beginner – Projects using Ribbed Patterns, shaping, finishing techniques, and assembly.

Ballerina Halter
64

Round Capelet
68

Fuzzy Jacket 72

Little Man
Cardigan 106

Resources

Manufacturers
Wholesale only. Contact companies for local retailers.

*Berroco, Inc.
P.O. Box 367
14 Elmdale Road
Uxbridge, MA 01569
tel: 508.278.2527

*Colinette Hand Dyed Yarns,
Distributed in the US by
Unique Kolours
28 N. Bacton Hill Road
Malvern, PA 19355
tel: 800.252.3934
www.uniquekolours.com

*Crystal Palace Yarns
160 23rd Street
Richmond, CA 94804
tel: 510.237.9988
www.straw.com

Filatura di Crosa
Distributed by Tahki.Stacy
Charles, Inc.

Gedifra Yarns
Knitting Fever, Inc.
315 Bayview Avenue
Amityville, NY 11701
tel: 516.546.3600
fax: 516.546.6871
www.knittingfever.com

Ironstone Yarns
P.O. Box 8
Las Vegas, NM 87701
tel: 800.343.4914
fax: 505.425.6967

Jelly Yarn™
Dimensional Illustrators, Inc.
362 Second Street Pike / #112
Southampton, PA 18966
tel: 215.953.1415
fax: 215.953.1697
www.yummy-yarns.com
email:yummyyarns@3dimillus.com

Katia Yarn
Distributed by Knitting Fever Inc.
(see Gedifra Yarns)

King Tut Yarn
Distributed by Halcyon Yarns
12 School Street
Bath, MA 04530
tel: 800.341.0282
www.halcyonyarn.com

Lion Brand Yarn
135 Kero Road
Carlstadt, NJ 07072
tel: 800.258.9276
www.lionbrand.com

Patons Yarns
320 Livingstone Avenue South
Listowel, Ont. Canada N4W 3H3
tel: 519.291.3780
www.patonsyarns.com

Plassard Yarns
Distributed by Brookman Imports
105 Dixon Drive
Chestertown, MD 21620
tel: 866.341.9425
www.Plassardyarnsusa.com

*Plymouth Yarn Company, Inc.
P.O. Box 28
Bristol, PA 19007
tel: 215.788.0459
www.plymouthyarn.com

*Schaefer Yarn Company
3514 Kelly's Corners Road
Interlaken, NY 14847
tel: 607.532.9452
www.schaeferyarn.com

*Skacel Collection, Inc.
P.O. Box 88110
Seattle, WA 98138-2110
8041 S. 180th Street
Kent, WA 98032
tel: 425.291.9600
fax: 425.291.9610
www.skacelknitting.com

*Trendsetter Yarns
16745 Saticoy Street / #101
Van Nuys, CA 91406
www.trendsetteryarns.com
tel: 818.780.5497

Knitting Consultants
Dr. Gail Cohen, Bala Cynwyd, PA

Maria Williams
Stitch Inn by Peddler's Village
5788 Route 202
Lahaska, PA 18931
tel: 215.794.4120

Candi Parente
The Knitting Room
26 S. Main Street
Medford, NJ 08055
tel: 609.654.9003

Contact Information
Nick and Kathleen Greco
Dimensional Illustrators, Inc.
362 Second Street Pike / #112
Southampton, PA 18966
tel: 215.953.1415
fax: 215.953.1697

Yarn Contributors

About the Authors

Since 1989, Kathleen and Nick Greco have published craft, knitting, and graphic arts books. A full-time knitwear designer and crafter, Kathleen has appeared regularly on HGTV, DIY and Lifetime Television. Their book-packaging design firm, Dimensional Illustrators, Inc., is located in Bucks County, Pennsylvania.

About the Photographer

Joe VanDeHatert is a Cincinnati-based advertising and commercial photographer with Studio V. Joe balances his time shooting fashion and product photos for a variety of companies, large and small.

Index